Editors
Lorin Klistoff, M.A.
Mara Guckian

Editorial Manager
Karen J. Goldfluss, M.S. Ed.

Editor in Chief
Sharon Coan, M.S. Ed.

Cover Artist
Sue Fullam

Art Coordinator
Denice Adorno

Creative Director
Elayne Roberts

Imaging
James Edward Grace

Product Manager
Phil Garcia

Publishers
Rachelle Cracchiolo, M.S. Ed.
Mary Dupuy Smith, M.S. Ed.

STANDARDIZED TEST PRACTICE FOR 3RD GRADE

Author

Charles J. Shields

Teacher Created Materials, Inc.
6421 Industry Way
Westminster, CA 92683
www.teachercreated.com
ISBN 1-57690-678-7
©2000 Teacher Created Materials, Inc.
Made in U.S.A.

Table of Contents

You have undoubtedly given plenty of tests during your years of teaching—unit tests, pop quizzes, final exams, and yes, standardized tests. As a professional educator, you know that standardized tests have taken on an importance greater than any of the others.

No one who understands children and the nature of learning would argue that a standardized test provides a measure of a child's understanding, a teacher's effectiveness, or a school's performance. It is merely a statistical snapshot of a group of children on a particular day. And there is no "generic child." Take a look at a girl named Joanna, for instance. Reluctant to speak during discussions or participate in group work, she's a whiz at taking tests and scores high on formal tests. However, Dion, in the seat beside her, is creative but impulsive. He dawdles during timed tests and sometimes fills in the wrong answer section. His score? It is no more a true indication of his ability than his doodles of motorcycle-riding monsters in the margins of his papers. Right now you are probably thinking of a Joanna or a Dion in your class.

However, schools must be accountable to their communities. Moreover, issues of equity and opportunity for children require that some method of checking all students' progress as objectively as possible be administered annually or even semi-annually. As a result, at the insistence of parents, school boards, state legislatures, and national commissions, standardized tests and their results are receiving more attention than at any other time during the last 35 years.

The purpose of this book is to help you and your students get better results on standardized tests. The exercises are grade-specific and based on the most recent versions of these testing instruments:

The California Achievement Tests
The Iowa Tests of Basic Skills
The Comprehensive Tests of Basic Skills
The Stanford Achievement Tests
The Metropolitan Achievement Tests
The Texas Assessment of Academic Skills

Exercise materials designed for this book reflect skills from curricula, grade-level tests, and test taking from the California Academic Standards Commission, the New York State Testing Program for Elementary and Intermediate Grades, the Texas Essential Knowledge and Skills Program, and the Board of Education for the Commonwealth of Virginia. Your students can expect to revisit much of the content in this book and the style in which questions are posed on these and other standardized tests.

About the Practice Tests

You will notice several things right away about the exercises.

1. The tests are arranged by curricular topics: word recognition, whole numbers, or geography, for example.

2. The exercises are short enough that you can integrate them into your teaching day. If, over the several weeks approaching a test date, you spend 20 minutes on test taking, your students will build confidence and increase their knowledge base in preparation for the actual test. Becoming familiar with testing formats and practicing on sample questions is one of the most effective ways to improve scores.

3. Examples of student-constructed responses to problems and questions have been included. Students must write, draw, or show their work to get credit for their answers.

The first two sections of the booklet—Practice Listening and Practice Guessing—emphasizes skills small children need to know to be good test takers. The other sections are divided according to subject area—Language Arts, Computer/Technology, Mathematics, Science, and Social Studies.

Ways to Increase Students' Confidence

- Downplay the importance of how many right answers versus how many wrong answers your students give. These exercises generally have the same purpose as drills in sports—to improve players' ability through regular practice. Fill the role of coach as students learn to hit the long ball.

- Give credit for reasonable answers. Encourage students to explain why they answered as they did. Praise thoughtfulness and good guesses. Surprise them by giving partial credit because their logic is persuasive. On some state-designed tests, credit is given for "almost right" answers.

- In your classroom, promote a positive, relaxed feeling about test taking. It might be wise, for example, to put off administering a planned practice from this booklet if your students are anxious or feeling overwhelmed about something. Use a little psychology in strengthening the association in their minds between test taking and opportunities to feel pleased about oneself.

Language Arts

Reading

Read and comprehend narrative and expository text.

Use punctuation, syntax, sentence and story meaning to decode words.

Interpret poetry and recognize stanza and rhyme.

Infer main ideas, lessons, or morals in a variety of prose.

Compare traits of characters.

Distinguish between fact and opinion.

Recognize author's use of figurative language.

Identify synonyms.

Understand and interpret maps, charts, and diagrams.

Spelling and Writing

Identify parts of and types of sentences.

Plan and judge about what to include in written products.

Attend to spelling, mechanics, and format in writing.

Recognize correct usage.

Experiment with word order.

Computer/Technology

Issues

Identify uses of technology in the community.

Recognize a person's rights of ownership of computer-related work.

Identify how telecommunications has changed the way people work and play.

Knowledge and Skills

Identify essential computer terms.

Identify the functions of the physical components of a computer system.

Identify word processing steps.

Interpret data on charts and graphs and make predictions.

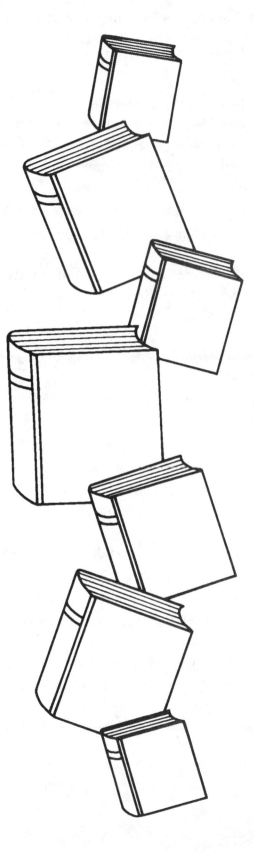

Mathematics

Whole numbers

Identify numbers to 1000 and beyond.

Compare and order numbers less than 1000.

Identify missing numbers.

Read and write word names for numerals.

Skip count by fives and tens.

Identify odd and even numbers.

Divide regions/sets into halves.

Describe relationship of parts to whole.

Solve problems, using addition and subtraction.

Tell missing addends for addition facts.

Solve multiple-digit addition and subtraction problems.

Use subtraction with zero.

Compute costs of items up to $5.00 and make change.

Use multiplication facts: 1s, 2s, 5s, 9s and 10s.

Geometric Ideas

Classify plane and solid figures.

Match congruent figures.

Recognize geometric figures in the environment.

Locate points on a coordinate grid; name with ordered pairs.

Classification and Pattern

Compare and describe similarities and differences.

Classify by more than one attribute.

Define and continue patterns in skip counting.

Identify classification and patterning in the environment.

Continue patterns of numerical sequences.

Find and correct errors in patterns.

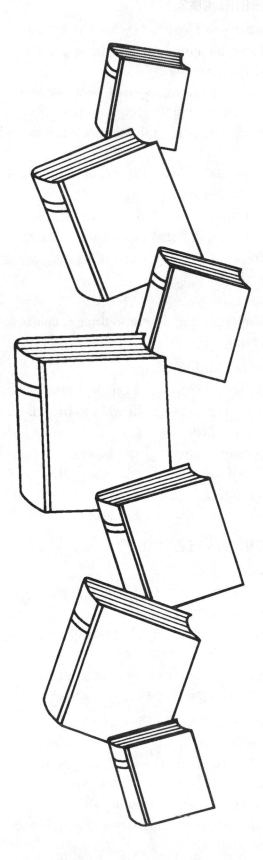

Mathematics *(cont.)*

Metric and Customary Measurement

Estimate length and height.

Estimate one inch and one centimeter.

Estimate number of smaller units contained in larger unit.

Weigh objects to nearest pound and kilogram.

Read Celsius and Fahrenheit thermometers.

Tell time to nearest minute.

Give value of sets of coins.

Read and write amounts of money in decimal form up to $5.00.

Solve simple time and money questions.

Locate points on a number line.

Problem Solving

Solve spatial visualization puzzles.

Estimate reasonable solutions.

Solve simple logic problems.

Use charts and graphs as sources of information.

Science

Process

Make observations based on the five senses.

Classify objects according to their properties.

Use amounts as a means of quantifying.

Estimate length, volume, mass, and temperature.

Make inferences to form conclusions.

Make predictions.

Support ideas by reference to evidence in texts.

Discriminate between cause and effect relationships.

Use space-time relations.

Make reasonable interpretations from data.

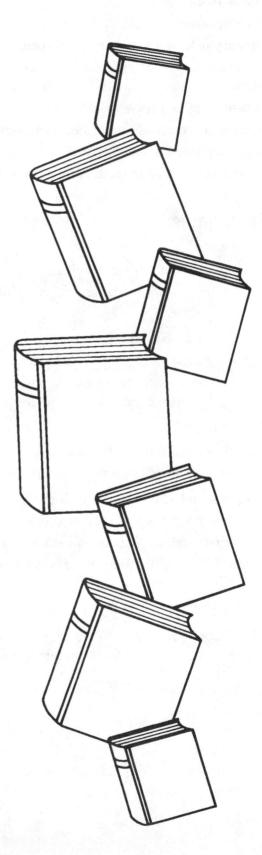

Science *(cont.)*

Life, Physical, and Earth Sciences

Identify characteristics of plants and animals.

Identify basic cycles affecting the earth.

Identify basic rock and soil types.

Identify characteristics of energy systems.

Identify solutions and mixtures.

Identify nutritional needs for a healthy body.

Social Studies

Citizenship

Identify attributes of good citizenship.

Describe appropriate behaviors in various environments.

Authority and Responsibility

Identify individuals who have authority.

Recognize consequences of responsible and irresponsible actions.

Government

Identify government bodies.

Identify examples of the elective process.

Religious and Cultural Traditions

Identify religious and secular symbols.

Identify symbols associated with holidays.

Identify selected famous people in history.

Geography

Describe uses of maps and globes.

Use geographic terms to describe landforms, bodies of water, weather, and climate.

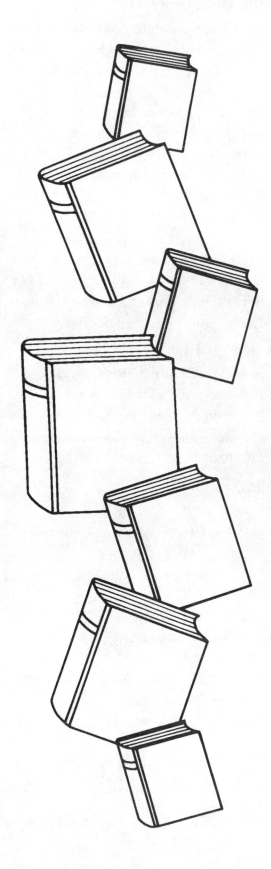

Marking Your Answers

In school, children take tests. Why? The reason is that your teacher, your parents, and school leaders such as the principal all want to know more about what you are learning in school. They can tell partly from your daily grades, from your reports, and from your work posted on the bulletin board in your classroom, but a test has its own, special purpose. The purpose of a test is to measure what you know and how you think.

A standardized test is one that is given to thousands and thousands of students. The writers of the questions try to be as fair as possible. After all, it would not mean anything if third-grade students took all kinds of tests—some easy, some hard. The results would be very confusing and meaningless. The scoring of standardized tests tries to be as fair as possible, too. It is done by a computer. However, for computer-scored tests, answer sheets must be marked the same way by all students. That is why everyone must use a pencil marked No. 2 and fill in the circles with dark marks.

Attention must also be paid to how a question is written. For example, a question on a standardized test might look like this:

Directions: Fill in the circle of your answer.

How do you write the plural of the word "mouse"?

mouses	mices	mice	meeses
Ⓐ	Ⓑ	Ⓒ	Ⓓ

You would fill in the circle under "mice." But what if the question were written this way?

Directions: Fill in the circle of your answer.

How do you write the plural of "house"?

Ⓐ hice

Ⓑ hices

Ⓒ hoose

Ⓓ houses

You would fill in the circle with a D beside "houses."

Marking Your Answers *(cont.)*

Of course, you will not fill in answers as soon as you are handed a standardized test. The first thing you will do is put your name on the answer sheet. Below is an example.

Each filled-in circle stands for a letter in someone's name. Figure out the person's name by looking at the filled-in circles and then writing the letter of the circle in the empty box above the row. Notice that the person filled in blank circles for spaces anywhere in her name, including leftover spaces at the end. Circles must be filled in under every box.

Did you figure out the person's name?

Last Name   **First Name**

(Name grid of bubbles, letters A–Z)

Why Practice Guessing?

Sometimes students will not answer a question on a test because they do not know the answer. Faced with choices that seem similar, they opt for no answer rather than choose a wrong answer. A second reason why students will leave a question blank is because the material is unfamiliar to them. In this case, students may think they do not know enough to make a choice at all.

Learning the process of elimination teaches students to rely on what they do know. The key to the process is finding information in a question, or set of answers, that is meaningful to the student. Students may not know what an igloo is, for example, but they can recognize a picture of an ordinary house and a doghouse—those cannot be igloos!

The questions in this section are slightly beyond a third grader's ability level. The purpose is to confront them with a term or a concept or a set of choices that are hard to understand. Emphasize to students that standardized tests are not usually this hard. Explain that they are learning how to get rid of answers that cannot be right.

In fact, it is not important that students choose the exact right answer to each question in this section. The goal is to get them to eliminate two obviously wrong choices. Two right answers will be given for each question in the teacher's script. The better answer of the two right answers will be underlined. It is a good idea to go over the questions and answers in the tests right away to reinforce students' understanding of how the process of elimination works.

Here's the Idea

Read the script on the next page to the children. This exercise encourages students to make good guesses at correct answers by using the process of elimination. Often, learning the process of elimination pleases students, because they discover their prior knowledge and experiences help them get rid of incorrect answers right away.

Teacher Script

Sometimes you have to guess on a test. You may think, "I don't know the answer to this question," or "I'm not sure of the answer." But you should always answer every question. You might have to guess. We are going to learn how to make good guesses.

Look at the page. (*Check to see that students are on the correct page.*) We are going to play a guessing game called "Which Animal is the Most Popular at the Zoo?" This is how we play. I will think of an animal. Then I will give you clues. You will listen and cross out the animal that cannot be the one I am thinking of.

Put your finger on the number 1. In this row there is a turtle, a lion, a giraffe, an elephant, and an ostrich. The animal I am thinking of has four feet. Which animal cannot be the one I am thinking of? (*the ostrich*) Cross it out.

Put your finger on the number 2. Now the ostrich is gone, and there is a turtle, a lion, a giraffe, and an elephant. The animal I am thinking of has a short neck. Which animal cannot be the one I am thinking of? (*the giraffe*) Cross it out. There are three animals left.

Put your finger on the number 3. Here are the three animals that are left. The animal I am thinking of does not have a shell. Which animal cannot be the one I am thinking of? (*the turtle*) Cross it out.

Put your finger on the number 4. There are two animals left. The animal I am thinking of has fur. Which animal cannot be the one I am thinking of? (*the elephant*) Cross it out.

So which animal is the most popular at the zoo? (*the lion*)

How did you figure out the animal I was thinking of? (*listened for clues; crossed-out some animals*) The more wrong answers you can get rid of, the easier it is to guess the right answer. Remember to answer every question on a test. Sometimes you will have to guess. But first, get rid of the answers you know are not right. This will make you a good guesser.

Which Animal is the Most Popular at the Zoo?

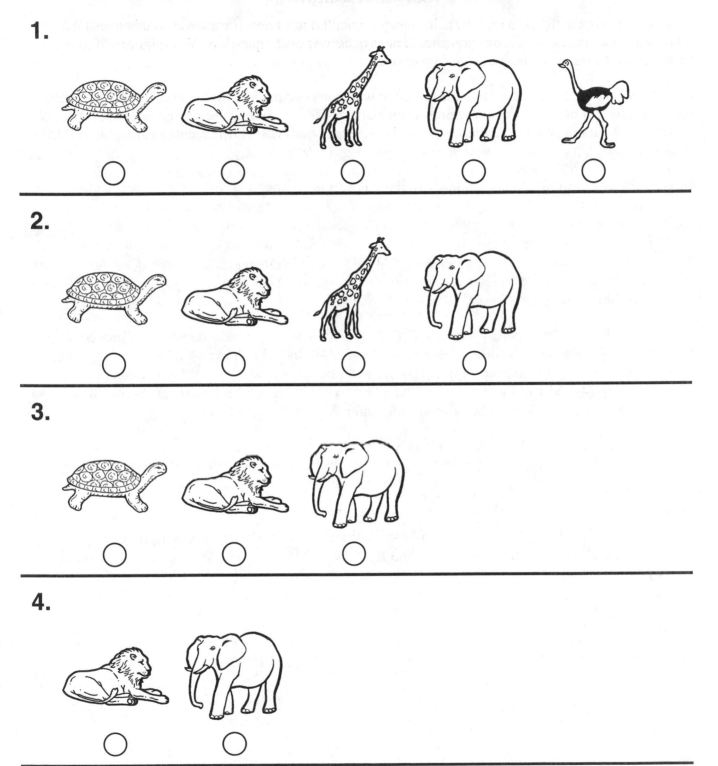

1.

2.

3.

4.

Teacher Script *(cont.)*

Now we have rows of four pictures again. We are going to practice getting rid of answers that cannot be right. This time the questions are hard. These questions are harder than the ones you will see on a real test. But I want you to get rid of two answers that cannot be right.

Go to row number 5. An accountant is someone who works inside an office. Which one is a picture of an accountant? Look at the four pictures. Remember what you learned about guessing. Get rid of two answers that cannot be right. This time, do not cross them out. Guess which answer is right. Fill in the circle of your guess. *(Pause.)* Which one did you guess? *(doctor or accountant)* Why did you get rid of the other two? *(The other two people are working outside and an accountant works inside.)* Remember to get rid of answers that cannot be right and then guess.

Now we are on number 6. I am going to ask you a question about this row. A whisk is very useful for making a cake. Which one is a whisk? Remember to get rid of two that cannot be right. *(Pause.)* Now guess and fill in the circle of your guess. Which one did you choose? *(the whisk or the scraper)* Why did you get rid of the other two? *(A screwdriver and a ball are not useful for making a cake.)* You are making good guesses now.

Look at number 7. This row has four numbers in it. Listen while I say the question. *(Pause.)* André is seven years old. His sister Tasha is two times older than André. How old is André 's sister? Get rid of two answers than cannot be right. Fill in the circle of your guess. *(Pause.)* Which number did you guess? *(12 or 14)* Why did you get rid of the other two? *(Because 5 and 2 are less than 7, and Tasha is older than André.)* Good guessing works for numbers or pictures, doesn't it?

Go to row number 8. This question is about a house. Mr. Anderson's roof has a gable that is 14 feet high. Which picture shows Mr. Anderson's gable? *(Pause.)* Guess and fill in the circle. Which one did you guess? *(the chimney or the gable)* Why did you get rid of the other two? *(You could not see a roof at all.)*

Now we are on number 9. This question is about shapes. Which picture shows a right triangle? *(Pause.)* Get rid of two. Make your guess and fill in the circle. *(Pause.)* Which one did you choose? *(the scalene or right triangle)* Why didn't you choose the other two? *(They are not triangles.)* Learning to be a good guesser is learning to get rid of answers that cannot be right.

Do you see the stop sign at the bottom of the page? Do not turn the page.

5.

Ⓐ   Ⓑ   Ⓒ   Ⓓ

6.

Ⓐ   Ⓑ   Ⓒ   Ⓓ

7.

14   12   5   2

Ⓐ   Ⓑ   Ⓒ   Ⓓ

8.

Ⓐ   Ⓑ   Ⓒ   Ⓓ

9.

Ⓐ   Ⓑ   Ⓒ   Ⓓ

STOP

Directions: Read the story and answer the questions.

Uncle Mitya's Horse

Uncle Mitya had a very fine horse. Some thieves heard about the horse and made plans to steal it. They came after dark and climbed over the fence into Uncle Mitya's yard. Now it happened that a farmer, who had a pet bear with him, came to spend the night at Uncle Mitya's house. Uncle Mitya took the farmer into the house. Then he let the horse out of the barn into the yard. He put the bear out there, too. The thieves came into the yard and began to feel around in the dark. The bear got on his hind legs and grabbed one of the thieves, who was so frightened he screamed with all his might. Uncle Mitya and the farmer came out and caught the thieves.

—Leo Tolstoy

1. Draw a picture that shows what is described in the story.

2. The conflict in this story is
   - (A) a farmer owns a dangerous bear.
   - (B) thieves want to steal Uncle Mitya's horse.
   - (C) where to put the bear for the night.
   - (D) the thieves sneak into the yard.

3. What do you think?
   - (A) Uncle Mitya wanted to catch the thieves.
   - (B) The farmer brought a bear to catch the thieves.
   - (C) The thieves tricked themselves into getting caught.
   - (D) The thieves thought they could get along with the bear.

4. A word that could describe Uncle Mitya is
   - (A) smart.
   - (B) mean.
   - (C) foolish.
   - (D) lucky.

Directions: Read the story and answer the questions.

Putting a Bell on the Cat

The mice could stand it no longer. From everywhere in the house they gathered in the Great Hall of Discussion, which was really a cardboard box by the water heater in the basement.

What was the reason for their meeting? What were they upset about? They needed to decide what to do about their great enemy, the cat!

"That cat is so dangerous, she'll destroy hundreds of us!" shouted one mouse angrily.

"Thousands!" agreed another.

"Millions!" declared a third.

"Order! Order!" demanded a fat mouse with a long tail. He drummed his foot thunderously on the water heater to get everyone's attention.

"Ahem!" he began at last, when all the mice had settled down. From the corner of the basement, a cricket watched with interest.

"We are here to discuss what to do about the cat," said the fat mouse.

"She must be stopped!" squeaked a frightened voice. It came from a young mouse who had barely escaped the cat's claws—claws that were as sharp as fishhooks.

"I agree," said the fat mouse. "We need protection from her. But what can we do?"

The fat mouse waited impatiently, but no one spoke.

"Well?" he asked.

In the corner, the cricket chirped.

"That's it!" cried one of the mice. He was thin and nervous looking from not daring to steal food from the kitchen for three weeks. "The cat is deadly because we can't hear her coming. We need to be able to hear her, you see?"

The mice all nodded. Yes, they understood.

"But how? What can we do to make the cat louder?" questioned the fat mouse.

"Tie a bell around her!" replied the thin mouse excitedly. "A bell on a collar around her neck. Every time she tries to sneak up on us, we'll hear the bell!"

The mice looked at each other and cheered. This was the best idea anyone had ever had for dealing with the cat. A bell! It was perfect!

They jumped up and down. The blue flame under the water heater made their shadows on the basement wall as big as kangaroos. The only mouse who wasn't acting overjoyed was an old mouse who shook his head sadly.

"All right, it's settled," said the fat mouse. "We'll tie a bell around the cat's neck, and we won't need to be afraid of her anymore. Now, who will volunteer to bell the cat?"

Silence. Most of the mice looked down, hoping not to be noticed.

Finally, the old mouse spoke up. "Yes, it's easy_____."

5. Finish what you think the old mouse said.
   - Ⓐ "Yes, it's easy to talk about the cat like this."
   - Ⓑ "Yes, it's easy to meet secretly."
   - Ⓒ "Yes, it's easy to suggest things no one will do."
   - Ⓓ "Yes, it's easy to act excited."

6. Where does this story happen?
   - Ⓐ in the kitchen
   - Ⓑ in the basement
   - Ⓒ around a campfire
   - Ⓓ long ago

7. Which is the best description of the plot of the story?
   - Ⓐ A cat is catching mice in a house.
   - Ⓑ Mice hold a meeting to decide what to do about a cat.
   - Ⓒ An old mouse tells young mice what to do.
   - Ⓓ A cricket gives mice an idea.

8. Which is an example of a comparison in the story?
   - Ⓐ From the corner of the basement, a cricket watched with interest.
   - Ⓑ In the corner, the cricket chirped.
   - Ⓒ The blue flame under the water heater made their shadows as big as kangaroos on the basement wall.
   - Ⓓ "Every time she tries to sneak up on us, we'll hear the bell!"

9. Which mouse has the idea for the bell?
   - Ⓐ the fat mouse
   - Ⓑ the mouse who was skinny from not daring to steal food from the kitchen for three weeks
   - Ⓒ the old mouse
   - Ⓓ a young mouse who had barely escaped the cat's claws–claws that were as sharp as fishhooks

10. When the mice say the cat will catch hundreds, thousands, millions of mice, this is an example of
    - Ⓐ plot.
    - Ⓑ exaggeration.
    - Ⓒ character.
    - Ⓓ author.

11. When "most of the mice looked down, hoping not to be noticed," it was because
    - Ⓐ they were embarrassed.
    - Ⓑ they were pleased.
    - Ⓒ they were waiting for the old mouse to speak.
    - Ⓓ they were afraid to be picked.

STOP

Directions: You will see three words. One of them does not rhyme with the other two. Fill in the circle of the word that does not rhyme. Here is a sample.

Sample	ate	great	taste
	Ⓐ	Ⓑ	Ⓒ

1.	said	head	sad
	Ⓐ	Ⓑ	Ⓒ

2.	eye	eat	pie
	Ⓐ	Ⓑ	Ⓒ

3.	nail	way	pale
	Ⓐ	Ⓑ	Ⓒ

4.	fair	bear	ear
	Ⓐ	Ⓑ	Ⓒ

5.	cheek	take	sneak
	Ⓐ	Ⓑ	Ⓒ

6.	my	weigh	stay
	Ⓐ	Ⓑ	Ⓒ

7.	money	mommy	funny
	Ⓐ	Ⓑ	Ⓒ

8.	sneeze	please	place
	Ⓐ	Ⓑ	Ⓒ

STOP

Directions: Read the poem. Answer the questions by writing in the blank or filling in the circle of the correct answer.

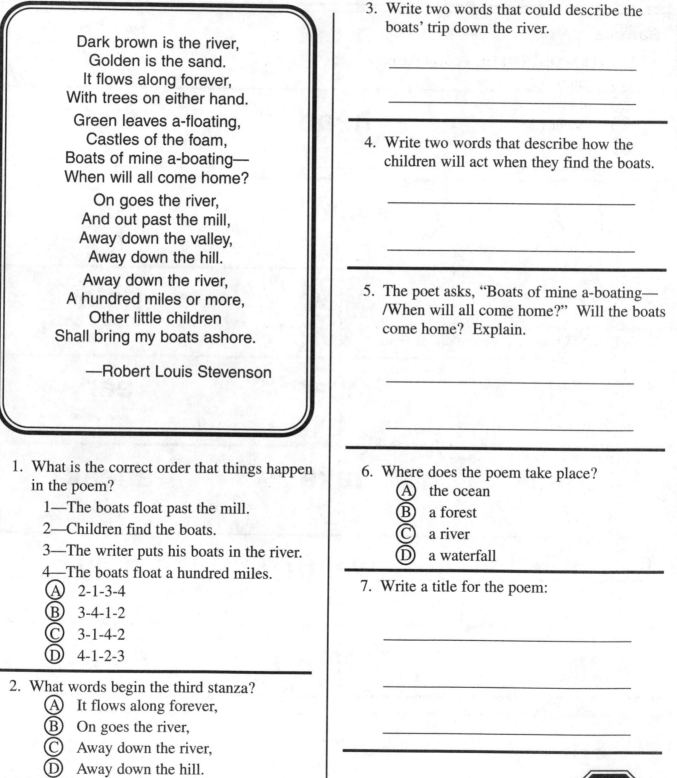

> Dark brown is the river,
> Golden is the sand.
> It flows along forever,
> With trees on either hand.
>
> Green leaves a-floating,
> Castles of the foam,
> Boats of mine a-boating—
> When will all come home?
>
> On goes the river,
> And out past the mill,
> Away down the valley,
> Away down the hill.
>
> Away down the river,
> A hundred miles or more,
> Other little children
> Shall bring my boats ashore.
>
> —Robert Louis Stevenson

1. What is the correct order that things happen in the poem?

    1—The boats float past the mill.

    2—Children find the boats.

    3—The writer puts his boats in the river.

    4—The boats float a hundred miles.

    Ⓐ 2-1-3-4

    Ⓑ 3-4-1-2

    Ⓒ 3-1-4-2

    Ⓓ 4-1-2-3

2. What words begin the third stanza?

    Ⓐ It flows along forever,

    Ⓑ On goes the river,

    Ⓒ Away down the river,

    Ⓓ Away down the hill.

3. Write two words that could describe the boats' trip down the river.

    _____

    _____

4. Write two words that describe how the children will act when they find the boats.

    _____

    _____

5. The poet asks, "Boats of mine a-boating— /When will all come home?" Will the boats come home? Explain.

    _____

    _____

6. Where does the poem take place?

    Ⓐ the ocean

    Ⓑ a forest

    Ⓒ a river

    Ⓓ a waterfall

7. Write a title for the poem:

    _____

    _____

STOP

Directions: You will read the sentences. One word or phrase will be in CAPITAL letters. Choose the word that has the same meaning.

Sample

We had a WONDERFUL view of the river.

- (A) sunny
- (B) ordinary
- (C) spectacular
- (D) dull

---

1. The long climb was DIFFICULT for Maggie.
   - (A) simple
   - (B) hard
   - (C) bumpy
   - (D) spread out

2. We RAISED the flag slowly up the pole.
   - (A) cheered
   - (B) looked at
   - (C) lifted up
   - (D) waved at

3. Ellen was ill. She was not IN CONDITION to play.
   - (A) the mood
   - (B) physically able
   - (C) seated
   - (D) cool enough

4. We watched a very old, SILENT movie.
   - (A) silly
   - (B) silver
   - (C) noisy
   - (D) soundless

5. The coach did not choose EITHER girl for pitcher.
   - (A) any
   - (B) one or the other
   - (C) that
   - (D) our

6. The sign said, "Use EXACT amount."
   - (A) any
   - (B) this
   - (C) precise
   - (D) exit

7. INSTEAD OF candy, we gave little toys on Halloween.
   - (A) with
   - (B) in place of
   - (C) because
   - (D) sometimes

8. I REMAINED in the tent by myself.
   - (A) stayed behind
   - (B) played
   - (C) cried
   - (D) thought

Directions: You will read a story, but sometimes a word is missing. You will choose which word is missing. Here is a sample.

Sample

Mr. Miller had a store. In his _____ he had things to buy.

    Ⓐ   Ⓑ   Ⓒ

   house **store** **room**

The Cat Who Ran Away

I had a cat. Its name was Dot. It was white and black.

One day Dot ran away. I was so _____. My mother said, "I have an

   Ⓐ   Ⓑ   Ⓒ

  happy **sad** **cry**

idea. We will put a _____ in the store. We will say, 'Dot is lost.

   Ⓐ Ⓑ Ⓒ

  name **cat** **picture**

Please_____ Dot for us'." I said, "Good _____!"

 Ⓐ Ⓑ Ⓒ   Ⓐ Ⓑ Ⓒ

feed **like** **find**   **dog** **day** **idea**

So we went to the store. There was a _____ for pictures. We did

   Ⓐ Ⓑ Ⓒ

  place **name** **light**

what mother said. Then we went _____.

   Ⓐ Ⓑ Ⓒ

  car **home** **other**

The Cat Who Ran Away *(cont.)*

That night, we had _____. The phone _____. My

        Ⓐ   Ⓑ   Ⓒ   Ⓐ   Ⓑ   Ⓒ

     dinner **sleep** **show**   **call** **rang** **stop**

mother talked to a lady on the phone. "She has found Dot!" my mother said.

We _____ to the lady's house. Dot was wet and _____.

Ⓐ   Ⓑ   Ⓒ   Ⓐ   Ⓑ   Ⓒ

on   **went** **are**   **dirty** **no** **sleep**

Dot said, "Meow! Meow!" We said _____ you to the lady. We went

                         Ⓐ   Ⓑ   Ⓒ

                        yes **take** **thank**

home. Now Dot is with us again.

Directions: You will answer questions about a picture you see. These pictures show information. You look at the picture or map and fill in the circle next to the answer you choose. Here is a sample.

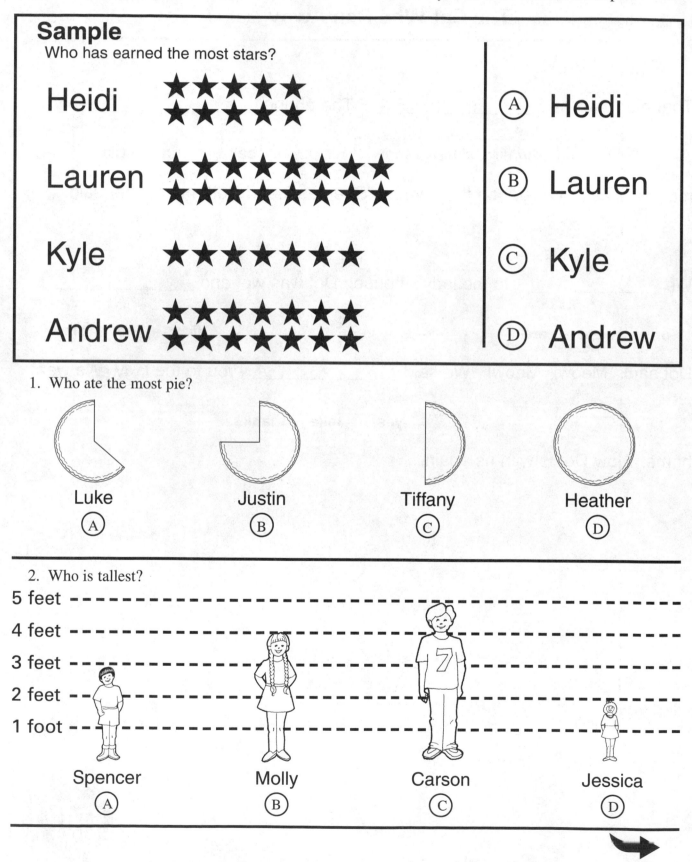

Sample

Who has earned the most stars?

Heidi

Lauren

Kyle

Andrew

- Ⓐ Heidi
- Ⓑ Lauren
- Ⓒ Kyle
- Ⓓ Andrew

1. Who ate the most pie?

Luke Ⓐ   Justin Ⓑ   Tiffany Ⓒ   Heather Ⓓ

2. Who is tallest?

5 feet
4 feet
3 feet
2 feet
1 foot

Spencer Ⓐ   Molly Ⓑ   Carson Ⓒ   Jessica Ⓓ

3. Who lives nearest the park?

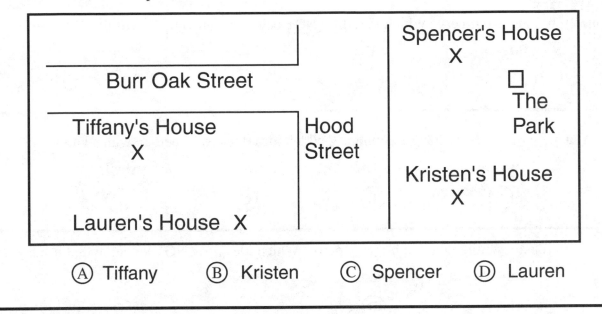

(A) Tiffany   (B) Kristen   (C) Spencer   (D) Lauren

4. Which city is farthest from Lake Michigan?

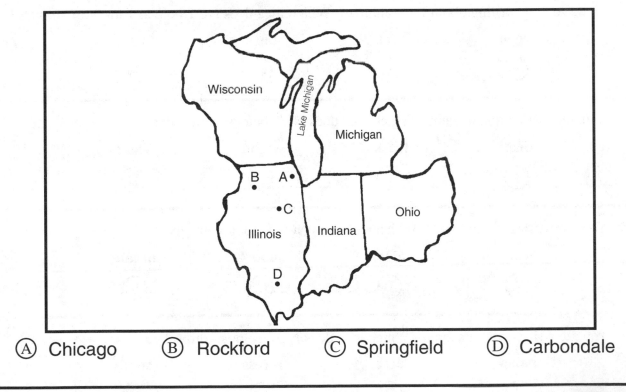

(A) Chicago   (B) Rockford   (C) Springfield   (D) Carbondale

Language Arts: Writing

Directions: You will answer questions about writing. Here is a sample.

Sample

You are writing about pets. Which idea does NOT belong when you are writing about pets?

food	water	bike	cage
(A)	(B)	(C)	(D)

---

1. You are writing about going swimming. Which idea does NOT belong with swimming?

waves	snow	sand	shells
(A)	(B)	(C)	(D)

---

2. Now, you are writing about a birthday party. Which idea does NOT belong with birthday party?

candles	cake	games	car
(A)	(B)	(C)	(D)

---

3. Now, you are writing about farm animals. Which idea does NOT belong with farm animals?

eggs	doll	barn	hay
(A)	(B)	(C)	(D)

---

4. You are writing about trains. Which idea does NOT belong with trains?

whistle	tracks	engine	shirt
(A)	(B)	(C)	(D)

---

5. You are writing about sleep. Which idea does NOT belong with sleep?

soap	night	pillow	dream
(A)	(B)	(C)	(D)

---

6. You are writing about school. Which idea does NOT belong with school?

paper	desk	recess	stone
(A)	(B)	(C)	(D)

STOP

Directions: Read the sentences. If a word is used incorrectly, fill in the circle by it. If there is no mistake, fill in C for "no mistake."

Samples

A.
- (A) Tim go to the corner
- (B) to wait for the bus.
- (C) no mistake

B.
- (A) My mother gave us five
- (B) dollars for the carnival.
- (C) no mistake

1.
- (A) The river runs south for
- (B) hundreds of miles.
- (C) no mistake

6.
- (A) We is proud to be on
- (B) the team from our class.
- (C) no mistake

2.
- (A) Lupe opened the lid
- (B) but there were nothing inside.
- (C) no mistake

7.
- (A) My sister Tasha she has
- (B) a game that's fun.
- (C) no mistake

3.
- (A) It took Robert three hours
- (B) to rake them leaves up.
- (C) no mistake

8.
- (A) Marsha is the only student
- (B) who can do ten pull-ups in a row.
- (C) no mistake

4.
- (A) Kent brung his drawing of
- (B) the moon to school.
- (C) no mistake

9.
- (A) Mom don't feel well.
- (B) She's sleeping late.
- (C) no mistake

5.
- (A) My sister hasn't never
- (B) gone to bed early.
- (C) no mistake

10.
- (A) My brother isn't in school,
- (B) but he ask a lot of questions!
- (C) no mistake

Directions: Read the sentence. Check the punctuation and capitalization. Fill in the circle for the capitalization or punctuation that needs to be added or changed to the underlined phrase. If no punctuation or capitalization is needed, fill in C for "none."

Samples

A. I forgot my <u>lunch Mom</u> brought it to me.

    Ⓐ .   Ⓑ ,   Ⓒ none

B. "<u>Marie!</u>" Andrew yelled from the shore. "Are you cold?"

    Ⓐ ,   Ⓑ .   Ⓒ none

1. Lupita, why don't you wait inside <u>for your ride</u>

    Ⓐ .   Ⓑ ?   Ⓒ none

2. <u>james</u> Hart Elementary School has 267 students.

    Ⓐ James   Ⓑ no period   Ⓒ none

3. Have you ever stood at the top of the Statue of <u>liberty</u>?

    Ⓐ Liberty   Ⓑ !   Ⓒ none

4. My grandfather was born <u>December 7</u> 1950.

    Ⓐ .   Ⓑ ,   Ⓒ none

5. "Run to first <u>base!</u>" the coach shouted.

    Ⓐ .   Ⓑ ?   Ⓒ none

6. Who wants this last piece of apple <u>pie</u>

    Ⓐ .   Ⓑ ?   Ⓒ none

Directions: Choose the sentence that sounds the best.

> **Sample**
> (A) Bobby, for a minute, would you come here?
> (B) For a minute would you come here, Bobby?
> (C) Bobby, would you come here for a minute?

1. (A) Malcolm goes in the room first always.
   (B) Malcolm always goes in the room first.
   (C) Malcolm first always goes in the room.

2. (A) The moon looks like a gold coin.
   (B) Like a gold coin the moon looks.
   (C) Looks like a gold coin the moon.

3. (A) Another day. Here comes sunshine.
   (B) For another day, here sunshine comes.
   (C) Here comes sunshine for another day.

4. (A) Walking in the city, exciting.
   (B) Walking in the city is exciting.
   (C) Exciting is walking in the city.

5. (A) Washington and Wells is the next stop.
   (B) The next stop Washington and Wells.
   (C) Washington and Wells the next stop.

6. (A) We camped all weekend by the beach.
   (B) By the beach all weekend we camped.
   (C) All weekend by the beach. We camped.

7. (A) For my dad sometimes, my dog Ginger does tricks.
   (B) Sometimes my dog, for my dad, does tricks.
   (C) My dog Ginger does tricks for my dad sometimes.

8. (A) In my room, I like to draw when it rains.
   (B) When it rains, I like to draw in my room.
   (C) I like to draw when it rains in my room.

Directions: Read the question. Fill in the circle of your answer.

1. What kind of sentence is this?

   ## Trees change color in the fall because there is less sunlight.

   (A) interrogative   (B) exclamatory   (C) declarative

2. What kind of sentence is this?

   ## Don't you think we should call Dad first?

   (A) interrogative   (B) exclamatory   (C) declarative

3. What kind of sentence is this?

   ## I don't think we should go to the park alone.

   (A) interrogative   (B) exclamatory   (C) declarative

4. What kind of sentence is this?

   ## Hide from Derek—he's coming!

   (A) interrogative   (B) exclamatory   (C) declarative

5. What is the subject of this sentence?

   ## The principal thanked us for our help.

   (A) thanked   (B) us   (C) principal

6. What is the predicate of this sentence?

   ## Five geese honked angrily at Jamie.

   (A) geese   (B) honked angrily at Jamie   (C) Jamie

7. What is the subject of this sentence?

   ## Should I ride the bus or walk?

   (A) bus   (B) ride the bus or walk   (C) I

8. What is the predicate of this sentence?

   ## I watched the game on TV with my cousins.

   (A) I   (B) on TV with my cousins   (C) watched the game on TV with my cousins

Directions: Below is a picture of a toy person someone made. Explain how you would make this toy, step-by-step. Then explain how you would use it. Give your writing a title.

_____

(title)

_____

_____

_____

_____

_____

_____

_____

Computer/Technology: Issues

Directions: You will see three pictures in each row. One of the pictures will show someone using technology. Fill in the circle below the picture of someone using technology.

1.
Ⓐ   Ⓑ   Ⓒ

2.
Ⓐ   Ⓑ   Ⓒ

3.
Ⓐ   Ⓑ   Ⓒ

4.
Ⓐ   Ⓑ   Ⓒ

5.
Ⓐ   Ⓑ   Ⓒ

6.
Ⓐ   Ⓑ   Ⓒ

7.
Ⓐ   Ⓑ   Ⓒ

Directions: Pretend that your school has these five rules about computers.

> ## Computer Rules
>
> - Respect other people.
> - Do not waste.
> - Do not lie.
> - Do not steal.
> - Do not destroy.

You will read about a student breaking one of the rules. You will decide which rule was broken. Here is a sample.

Sample

One day, Tamika set the printer on 100 copies. Then she left her seat at the computer. No one knew who made 100 copies. Which rule did Tamika break? Fill in the circle next to your answer.

Do not steal.	Do not waste.	Respect other people.
Ⓐ	Ⓑ	Ⓒ

---

1. Arthur is angry at Jason. He took Jason's disk and erased it. Then he put it back on Jason's desk. Which rule was broken?

Do not waste.	Do not lie.	Do not destroy.
Ⓐ	Ⓑ	Ⓒ

---

2. Angela found a good story on her computer that someone else had written. She copied it. She put her name at the top and handed it in.

Do not destroy.	Do not lie.	Do not steal.
Ⓐ	Ⓑ	Ⓒ

3. Paul doesn't like a boy in another class. He sends messages to the other boy's computer everyday, making fun of him. Which rule is being broken?

Respect other people.   Do not lie.   Do not waste.

Ⓐ   Ⓑ   Ⓒ

4. Tommy borrows Spencer's game disks for Monster Trucks. Tommy makes copies of them at home. He tells Spencer he will erase the game if he doesn't like it or buy the game if he does. What rule is being broken?

Do not steal.   Do not lie.   Do not waste.

Ⓐ   Ⓑ   Ⓒ

5. Sandra writes to students at other schools on her computer. She tells them that she is the teacher. She pretends that she is. What rule is being broken?

Respect other people.   Do not lie.   Do not destroy.

Ⓐ   Ⓑ   Ⓒ

6. Susan is writing a private letter on her computer. She only wants her teacher to see it. But Vanessa looks over Susan's shoulder. She tells other students what Susan is writing. What rule is being broken?

Do not destroy.   Do not waste.   Respect other people.

Ⓐ   Ⓑ   Ⓒ

Computer/Technology: Knowledge and Skills

Directions: Read the questions about computers. Choose your answer.

1. Which part of the computer do you use to move the cursor on the screen and click? Fill in the circle next to the picture.

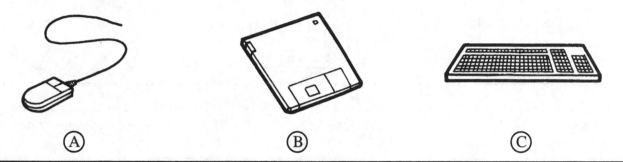

Ⓐ   Ⓑ   Ⓒ

2. What part of the computer do you look at while your are writing?

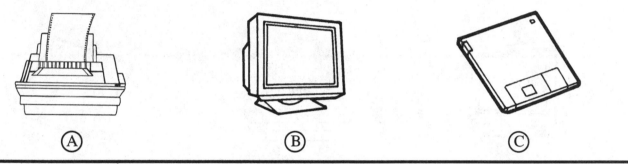

Ⓐ   Ⓑ   Ⓒ

3. When a message appears on the screen, what does it look like?

Do you want to save this box?

Ⓐ   Ⓑ   Ⓒ

4. What do you use to write on the computer screen?

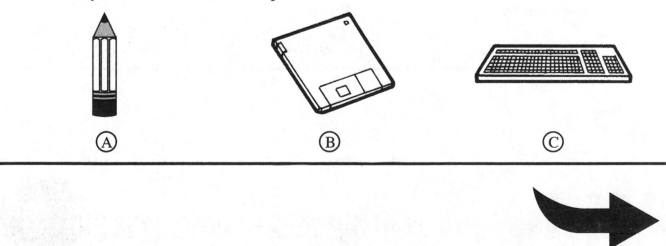

Ⓐ   Ⓑ   Ⓒ

5. What do you use to store your work?

Ⓐ   Ⓑ   Ⓒ

6. When you want a paper copy of your work, what does the paper come out of?

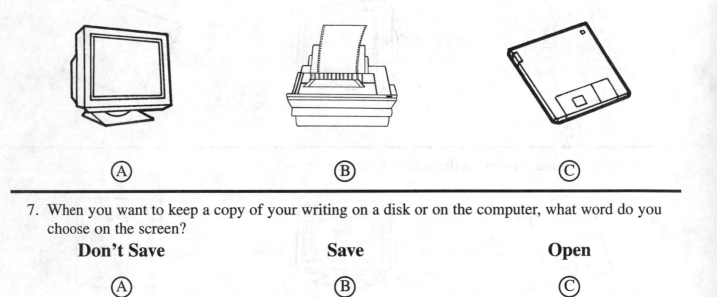

Ⓐ   Ⓑ   Ⓒ

7. When you want to keep a copy of your writing on a disk or on the computer, what word do you choose on the screen?

    Don't Save   **Save**   **Open**

       Ⓐ   Ⓑ   Ⓒ

8. When you want to end what you're doing on the computer, what word do you choose on the screen?

    Close or Exit   **Paste**   **Copy**

       Ⓐ   Ⓑ   Ⓒ

Computer/Technology: Knowledge and Skills *(cont.)*

Directions: Parker Elementary School is having a magazine sale. They are raising money for their trip to Chicago. Here is a spreadsheet about the magazines they sold. Read the questions. Fill in the circle next to your answer.

	A	B	C	D
1	**Magazine**	**Number Sold**	**Subscription Rate for 1 Year**	**Total Amount**
2	*Time*	15	$52.00	$780.00
3	*Newsweek*	7	$43.25	$302.75
4	*TV Guide*	11	$47.00	$517.00
5	*Redbook*	6	$22.25	$133.50
6	*Sports Illustrated*	27	$24.50	$661.50

1. The most subscriptions were sold for which magazine?

   (A) *TV Guide*   (B) *Time*   (C) *Newsweek*   (D) *Sports Illustrated*

2. The total amount of money taken in for each magazine is shown in which column?

   (A) Column A   (B) Column B   (C) Column C   (D) Column D

3. Where is the total amount for the sale of *TV Guide* shown?

   (A) B4   (B) D4   (C) C4   (D) A4

4. Where is the subscription rate for *Redbook* shown?

   (A) B5   (B) C5   (C) D5   (D) A5

Mathematics: Whole Numbers

Directions: This part of the test is about mathematics. Most of the questions in this section are about number patterns. Read each question. Fill in the circle of your answer. Here is a sample.

Sample

Which number comes next?

3, 5, 7, ___

Ⓐ 8
Ⓑ 12
Ⓒ 9
Ⓓ 10

---

1. One of the numbers is missing. Which one? Fill in the circle next to the number that is missing.

205   206   ___   208

Ⓐ 204
Ⓑ 209
Ⓒ 202
Ⓓ 207

---

2. There is a missing number in this row. Fill in the circle next to the number that is missing.

391   ___   393   394

Ⓐ 395
Ⓑ 300
Ⓒ 392
Ⓓ 390

---

3. There is a missing number in this row, too. Fill in the circle next to the number that is missing.

___   198   199   200

Ⓐ 196
Ⓑ 197
Ⓒ 190
Ⓓ 299

---

4. Which number is missing in this row? Fill in the circle next to the number that is missing.

797   798   799   ___

Ⓐ 801
Ⓑ 800
Ⓒ 710
Ⓓ 701

---

5. Which number is missing in this row? Fill in the circle next to the number that is missing.

22   24   26   ___

Ⓐ 29
Ⓑ 20
Ⓒ 28
Ⓓ 27

---

6. Which number is missing in this row? Fill in the circle next to the number that is missing.

15   ___   25   30

Ⓐ 16
Ⓑ 20
Ⓒ 5
Ⓓ 25

7. Which number is missing in this row? Fill in the circle next to the number that is missing.

10   20   ___   40

Ⓐ 10
Ⓑ 30
Ⓒ 50
Ⓓ 25

8. Which number is missing in this row? Fill in the circle next to the number that is missing.

518   ___   522   524

Ⓐ 519
Ⓑ 521
Ⓒ 520
Ⓓ 517

9. Which number is missing in this row? Fill in the circle next to the number that is missing.

399   402   405   ___

Ⓐ 407
Ⓑ 408
Ⓒ 409
Ⓓ 406

10. Which number is missing in this row? Fill in the circle next to the number that is missing.

417   ___   431   438

Ⓐ 424
Ⓑ 249
Ⓒ 422
Ⓓ 430

11. There is a number missing at the question mark. Which number is it? Fill in the circle next to the answer you choose.

30   35   ___   45   50   55   60

Ⓐ 37
Ⓑ 40
Ⓒ 4
Ⓓ 50

12. There is a number missing at the question mark. Which number is it? Fill-in the circle next to the answer you choose.

105 110 115   ___   125 130 140

Ⓐ 110
Ⓑ 116
Ⓒ 120
Ⓓ 125

13. Which group has an odd number of toys? Fill in the circle of your answer.

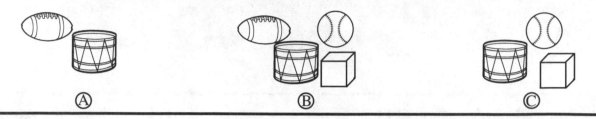

Ⓐ Ⓑ Ⓒ

14. Here are eight bicycles. Half of them need to be fixed. How many need to be fixed? Fill in the circle next to your answer.

Ⓐ 6
Ⓑ 4
Ⓒ 3

15. There are four pairs of children. Half the children are going on a field trip. How many children are going on a field trip?

Ⓐ 8
Ⓑ 2
Ⓒ 4

16. There are four sandwiches and six plates. If the sandwiches are cut in half and each half is put on a plate, how many sandwich halves will be left over?

Ⓐ 4
Ⓑ 5
Ⓒ 2

17. Carson helped make an apple pie. She took three quarters of it to her grandmother. Which picture shows what is left?

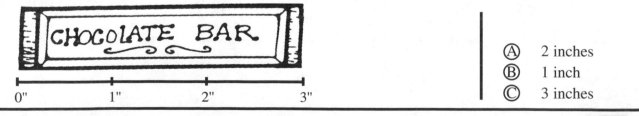

Ⓐ Ⓑ Ⓒ

18. This candy bar is three inches long. Luke cut off one-third of it. How much is left?

Ⓐ 2 inches
Ⓑ 1 inch
Ⓒ 3 inches

Directions: On this part of the test, you will do some more addition and subtraction. Read each question. Fill in the circle of your answer. You may work the problems on another piece of paper.

1. How much is X? Fill in the circle of your answer.

$$25 + X = 19$$

Ⓐ 7
Ⓑ 14
Ⓒ 6

2. How much is X? Fill in the circle of your answer.

$$X + 35 = 45$$

Ⓐ 15
Ⓑ 10
Ⓒ 14

3. If we know that X = 5, how much is Y? Fill in the circle of your answer.

$$X + Y = 8$$

Ⓐ 2
Ⓑ 7
Ⓒ 3

4.

$$3 + 2 + 1 =$$

Ⓐ 6
Ⓑ 5
Ⓒ 7

5.
$$\begin{array}{r} 15 \\ 20 \\ +\ 3 \\ \hline \end{array}$$

Ⓐ 33
Ⓑ 48
Ⓒ 38

6.
$$\begin{array}{r} 10 \\ +\ 11 \\ \hline \end{array}$$

Ⓐ 20
Ⓑ 12
Ⓒ 21

7.
$$\begin{array}{r} 15 \\ +\ 13 \\ \hline \end{array}$$

Ⓐ 28
Ⓑ 29
Ⓒ 18

8.

$$26 - 22 =$$

Ⓐ 28
Ⓑ 4
Ⓒ 3

9.
$$
\begin{array}{r} 21 \\ -10 \\ \hline \end{array}
$$

11	20	31
Ⓐ	Ⓑ	Ⓒ

10.
$$
\begin{array}{r} 83 \\ +15 \\ \hline \end{array}
$$

98	78	62
Ⓐ	Ⓑ	Ⓒ

11.
$$
\begin{array}{r} 411 \\ +188 \\ \hline \end{array}
$$

377	399	599
Ⓐ	Ⓑ	Ⓒ

12.
$$
\begin{array}{r} 15 \\ +10 \\ \hline \end{array}
$$

5	15	25
Ⓐ	Ⓑ	Ⓒ

13.
$$
\begin{array}{r} 315 \\ -100 \\ \hline \end{array}
$$

300	215	200
Ⓐ	Ⓑ	Ⓒ

14. What is the next number: 30, 300, 3000, _____.

3,003	900	30,000
Ⓐ	Ⓑ	Ⓒ

15. If you place a zero between the ten's place and the one's place in the number 393, the new number is _____.

Ⓐ   three thousand one hundred and ninety-three
Ⓑ   three thousand nine hundred three
Ⓒ   three thousand ninety three

16. What is another way to write 4 thousands 8 tens 2 ones?

48	4,082	40,082
Ⓐ	Ⓑ	Ⓒ

17. In which number does the 7 stand for hundreds?

7,512	5,173	3,741
Ⓐ	Ⓑ	Ⓒ

18. Which number is greater than 5,836?

5,880	5,386	5,835
Ⓐ	Ⓑ	Ⓒ

19. Which is the number for four thousand seventy-five?

4,175	4,075	4,750
Ⓐ	Ⓑ	Ⓒ

20.
$$\begin{array}{r} 5 \\ \times\,4 \\ \hline \end{array}$$

9	15	20
Ⓐ	Ⓑ	Ⓒ

21.
$$1 \times 5 \times 2 =$$

5	10	12
Ⓐ	Ⓑ	Ⓒ

22.
$$3 \times 3 =$$

6	12	9
Ⓐ	Ⓑ	Ⓒ

23.
$$\begin{array}{r} 4 \\ \times\,2 \\ \hline \end{array}$$

8	2	6
Ⓐ	Ⓑ	Ⓒ

24.
$$2 \times 5 \times 4 =$$

11	40	28
Ⓐ	Ⓑ	Ⓒ

25.
$$\begin{array}{r} 2 \\ \times\,9 \\ \hline \end{array}$$

16	19	18
Ⓐ	Ⓑ	Ⓒ

➡

Directions: Use this snack shop menu for questions 26–30.

French fries. . . . . 50¢

Juice box . . . . 75¢

Hamburger. $1.00

Hot dog . . . . 90¢

Pop. 60¢

26. Marsha bought a hot dog and pop. She paid $2.00. How much is her change?

      75¢   50¢   55¢

      Ⓐ   Ⓑ   Ⓒ

27. Andrew bought french fries, a juice box, and a hamburger. How much does he owe?

      $2.25 $2.00 $2.05

      Ⓐ   Ⓑ   Ⓒ

28. Kyle bought a juice box and paid $1.00. How much is his change?

      50¢   30¢   25¢

      Ⓐ   Ⓑ   Ⓒ

29. Arthur bought a hamburger and a hot dog. He paid $2.00. How much is his change?

      10¢   5¢   25¢

      Ⓐ   Ⓑ   Ⓒ

30. Mr. Anderson bought three hamburgers. He paid $5.00. What is his change?

      $3.00 $1.00 $2.00

      Ⓐ   Ⓑ   Ⓒ

Mathematics: Geometric Ideas

Directions: This part of the test will be about shapes. Read each question, and fill in the circle of your answer. Here is a sample.

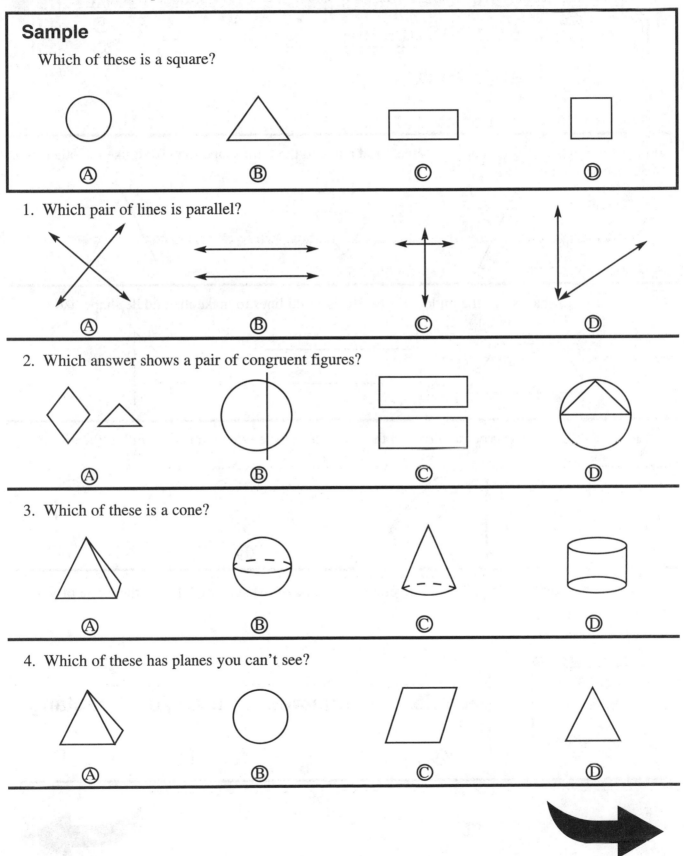

Sample

Which of these is a square?

Ⓐ   Ⓑ   Ⓒ   Ⓓ

1. Which pair of lines is parallel?

Ⓐ   Ⓑ   Ⓒ   Ⓓ

2. Which answer shows a pair of congruent figures?

Ⓐ   Ⓑ   Ⓒ   Ⓓ

3. Which of these is a cone?

Ⓐ   Ⓑ   Ⓒ   Ⓓ

4. Which of these has planes you can't see?

Ⓐ   Ⓑ   Ⓒ   Ⓓ

5. Use the figure. What is the location of point A?

Ⓐ (1,2)
Ⓑ (1,1)
Ⓒ (2,2)
Ⓓ (2,1)

6. Here are two shapes that are the same. Add a line to the third shape to make it like the other two. Draw right on your page.

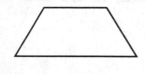

7. Here are two shapes. In the middle are two lines. Add lines to make the middle shape like the other two. Draw right on your page.

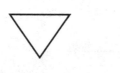

8. Here is a shape. If you put a mirror on the line, what shape would you see? Fill in the circle of your answer.

Ⓐ   Ⓑ   Ⓒ

9. Look at the suitcase. Which word describes the shape of the suitcase? Fill in the circle of your answer.

circle   **square**   **triangle**   **rectangle**

Ⓐ   Ⓑ   Ⓒ   Ⓓ

10. Look at the picture of the plate, the clock, and the ball. With which group of shapes do they belong? Fill in the circle of your answer.

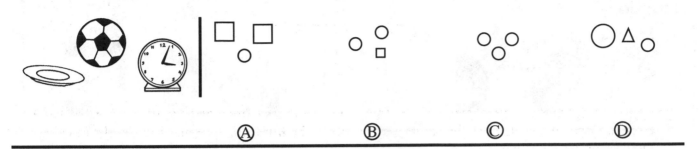

Ⓐ   Ⓑ   Ⓒ   Ⓓ

11. Look at the picture of the book, the board game, and the mat. With which group of shapes do they belong? Fill in the circle of your answer.

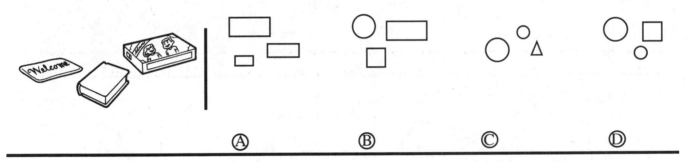

Ⓐ   Ⓑ   Ⓒ   Ⓓ

12. Here is a group of four small squares that are partly black and partly white. Next is another group of three squares. Choose a square that would makc both groups the same.

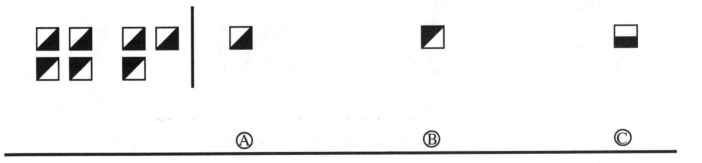

Ⓐ   Ⓑ   Ⓒ

Mathematics: Classification and Pattern

Directions: This part of the test is about patterns. Read each question, and fill in the circle of your answer. Here is a sample.

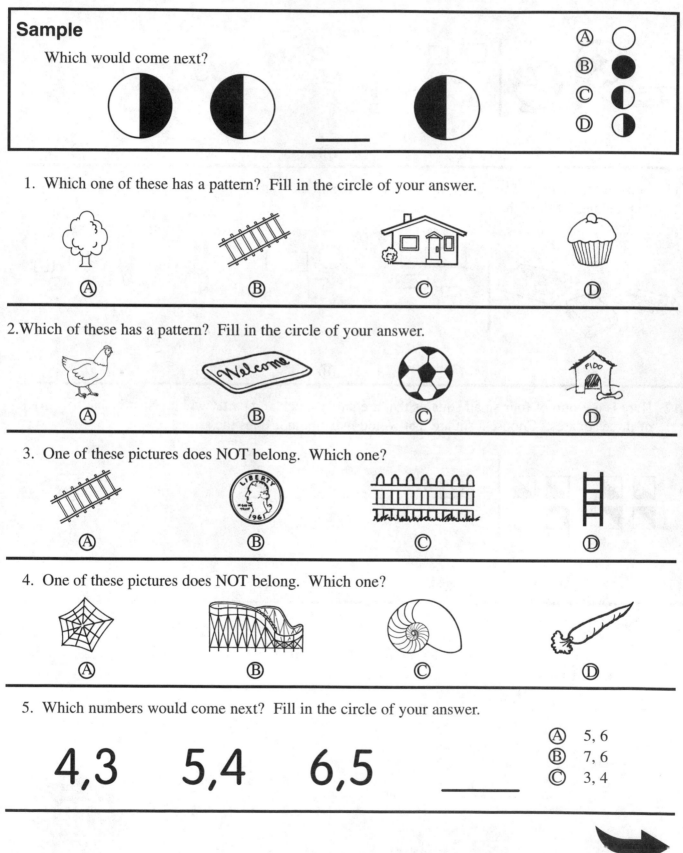

Sample

Which would come next?

Ⓐ ○
Ⓑ ●
Ⓒ ◐
Ⓓ ◑

1. Which one of these has a pattern? Fill in the circle of your answer.

Ⓐ   Ⓑ   Ⓒ   Ⓓ

2. Which of these has a pattern? Fill in the circle of your answer.

Ⓐ   Ⓑ   Ⓒ   Ⓓ

3. One of these pictures does NOT belong. Which one?

Ⓐ   Ⓑ   Ⓒ   Ⓓ

4. One of these pictures does NOT belong. Which one?

Ⓐ   Ⓑ   Ⓒ   Ⓓ

5. Which numbers would come next? Fill in the circle of your answer.

4,3   5,4   6,5   ____

Ⓐ 5, 6
Ⓑ 7, 6
Ⓒ 3, 4

6. Which numbers would come next? Fill in the circle of your answer.

3,6,9   6,9,12   9,12,15 ____

Ⓐ 9, 12, 18
Ⓑ 3, 6, 15
Ⓒ 12, 15, 18

7. Which number does NOT belong? Fill in the circle of your answer.

3   5   4   7   5   10

Ⓐ 10
Ⓑ 5
Ⓒ 3

8. Which number belongs in the blank? Fill in the circle of your answer?

10/5   12/6   14/7   16/__

Ⓐ 6
Ⓑ 9
Ⓒ 8

9. Which dice should come next? Fill in the circle next to your answer.

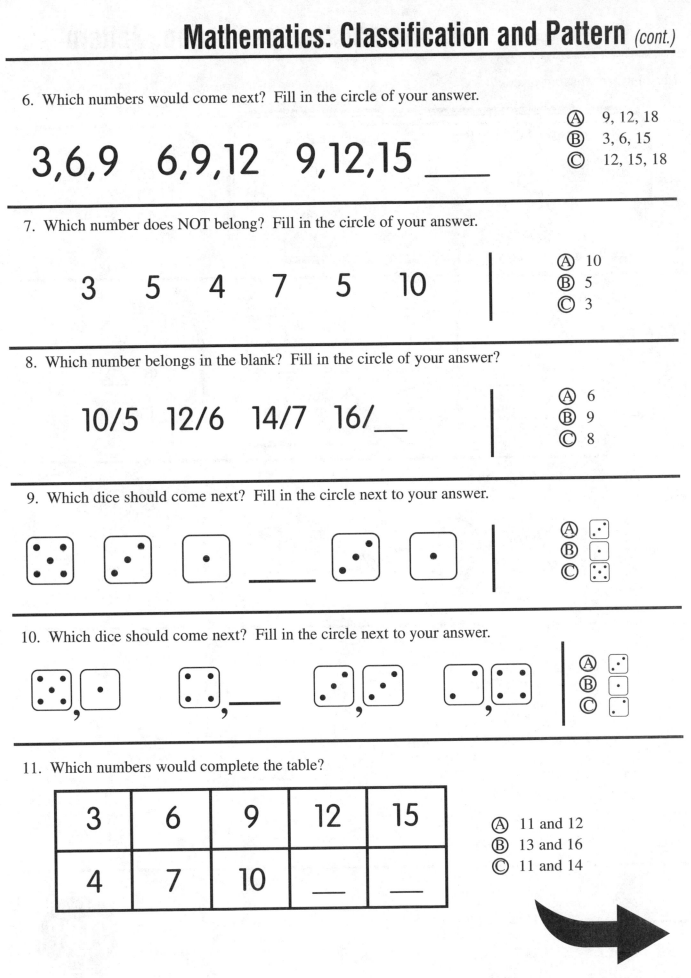

10. Which dice should come next? Fill in the circle next to your answer.

11. Which numbers would complete the table?

3	6	9	12	15
4	7	10	__	__

Ⓐ 11 and 12
Ⓑ 13 and 16
Ⓒ 11 and 14

12. Find the missing price.

Number of Candy Bars	Final Price
10	$3.00
11	$3.30
12	$3.60
13	$_____

Ⓐ $4.00
Ⓑ $3.80
Ⓒ $3.90

13. Which would come next?

Ⓐ ◯
Ⓑ △
Ⓒ ☐

14. Which belongs in the blank?

Ⓐ nickel
Ⓑ dime
Ⓒ quarter

15. Which clock comes next?

Ⓐ
Ⓑ
Ⓒ

Mathematics: Metric and Customary Measurement

Directions: In this part of the test, you will answer questions about measurement, time, and money. Read each question, and fill in the circle of your answer. Here is a sample.

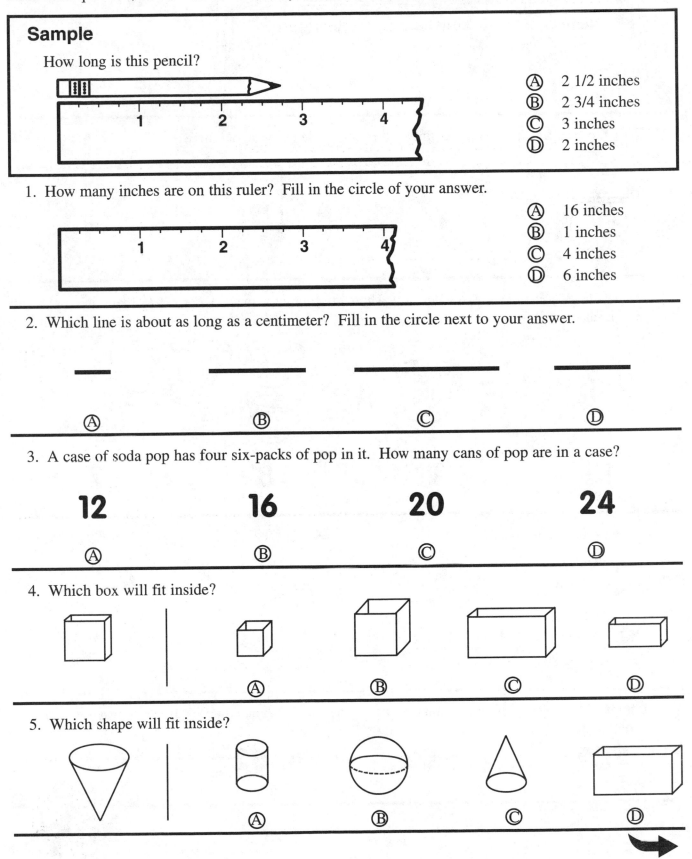

Sample

How long is this pencil?

- Ⓐ 2 1/2 inches
- Ⓑ 2 3/4 inches
- Ⓒ 3 inches
- Ⓓ 2 inches

1. How many inches are on this ruler? Fill in the circle of your answer.

- Ⓐ 16 inches
- Ⓑ 1 inches
- Ⓒ 4 inches
- Ⓓ 6 inches

2. Which line is about as long as a centimeter? Fill in the circle next to your answer.

Ⓐ   Ⓑ   Ⓒ   Ⓓ

3. A case of soda pop has four six-packs of pop in it. How many cans of pop are in a case?

12   **16**   **20**   **24**

Ⓐ   Ⓑ   Ⓒ   Ⓓ

4. Which box will fit inside?

Ⓐ   Ⓑ   Ⓒ   Ⓓ

5. Which shape will fit inside?

Ⓐ   Ⓑ   Ⓒ   Ⓓ

Mathematics: Metric and Customary Measurement *(cont.)*

6. Which one is a Celsius thermometer showing the freezing point of water?

7. Which one is for measuring height? Fill in the circle next to your answer.

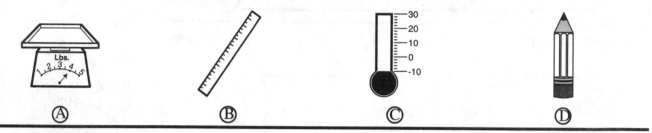

8. It takes three juice glasses to fill a cup. There are four cups in a pitcher. How many juice glasses will it take to fill the pitcher?

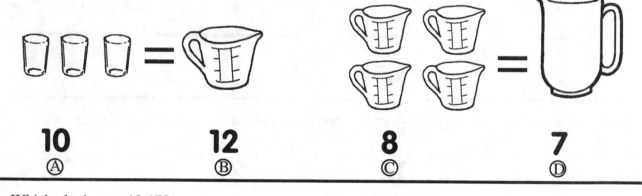

10
Ⓐ

12
Ⓑ

8
Ⓒ

7
Ⓓ

9. Which clock says 10:17?

Ⓐ   Ⓑ   Ⓒ   Ⓓ

10. Lauren's dad told her to come home at 4:55. She was 7 minutes late. What time was it when she came home?

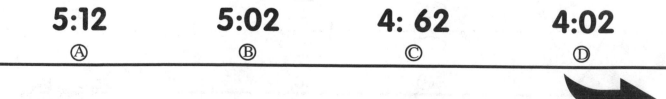

5:12
Ⓐ

5:02
Ⓑ

4: 62
Ⓒ

4:02
Ⓓ

Mathematics: Metric and Customary Measurement *(cont.)*

11. Which is four dollars and twenty-seven cents?

    Ⓐ 4.27¢   Ⓒ $40027
    Ⓑ $427   Ⓓ $4.27

12. How do you write $3.12?

    Ⓐ three twelve   Ⓒ three point twelve cents
    Ⓑ three dollars and twelve cents Ⓓ dollars three and twelve

13. Mark cuts the grass for one dollar an hour. He worked from two o'clock to five o'clock. How much did he earn?

    Ⓐ $4.00   Ⓒ $3.00
    Ⓑ $2.00   Ⓓ $7.00

14. Lupita baby-sits for two dollars an hour. She baby-sat from 6:00 to 8:30. How much did she earn?

    Ⓐ $4.00   Ⓒ $28.00
    Ⓑ $4.50   Ⓓ $5.00

15. Which group is closest in amount to one dollar?

    Ⓐ   Ⓑ   Ⓒ   Ⓓ

16. Libbie's bed is four feet wide. How many yards is that?

    Ⓐ four
    Ⓑ one yard and one foot
    Ⓒ two yards
    Ⓓ one yard and three feet

17. Pretend this is a subtraction problem. Fill the circle next to your answer.

    ⬤ − ⬤ = _____   Ⓐ 1 penny
                           Ⓑ 4 pennies
                           Ⓒ 1 dime
                           Ⓓ 1 nickel

Mathematics: Metric and Customary Measurement (cont.)

18. Pretend this a subtraction problem. Fill the circle next to your answer.

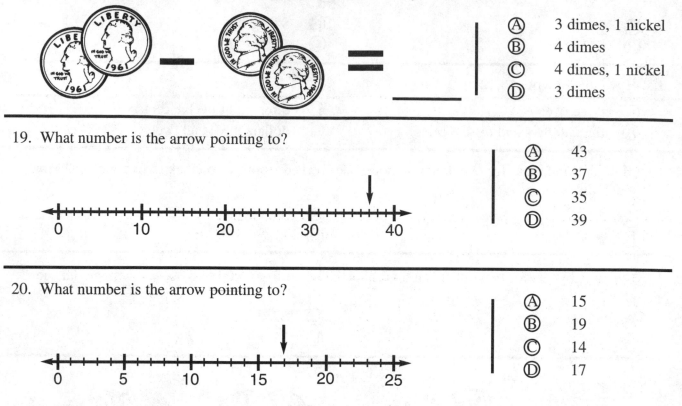

- Ⓐ 3 dimes, 1 nickel
- Ⓑ 4 dimes
- Ⓒ 4 dimes, 1 nickel
- Ⓓ 3 dimes

19. What number is the arrow pointing to?

- Ⓐ 43
- Ⓑ 37
- Ⓒ 35
- Ⓓ 39

20. What number is the arrow pointing to?

- Ⓐ 15
- Ⓑ 19
- Ⓒ 14
- Ⓓ 17

21. Angela bought a candy bar at the movies. She gave the boy at the counter four quarters. He gave her two dimes back. How much did the candy bar cost?

- Ⓐ $.75
- Ⓑ $.80
- Ⓒ $1.20
- Ⓓ $.64

22. What is the total value of these coins?

- Ⓐ $.44
- Ⓑ $.36
- Ⓒ $.54
- Ⓓ $.64

23. If July 4th is on a Wednesday, what day of the week will July 11th be?

Ⓐ Tuesday
Ⓑ Wednesday
Ⓒ Monday
Ⓓ Thursday

24. About how tall is a regular door?

Ⓐ 72 inches
Ⓑ 7 feet
Ⓒ 12 feet
Ⓓ 12 inches

25. How many degrees difference are there between thermometer A and B?

Ⓐ 24 degrees
Ⓑ 26 degrees
Ⓒ 8 degrees
Ⓓ 40 degrees

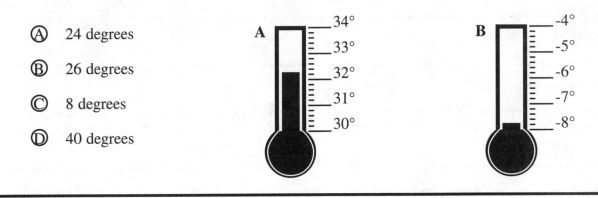

26. There are 2.54 centimeters in an inch. About how many centimeters are there in 10 inches?

Ⓐ 10
Ⓑ 25.4
Ⓒ 254
Ⓓ 2540

STOP

Mathematics: Problem Solving

Directions: This part of the test asks puzzle questions. Read each question, and fill in the circle of your answer. Here is a sample.

Sample

Three friends have six ice cream bars. They want to share. How many ice cream bars should each friend get?

Ⓐ 3
Ⓑ 1
Ⓒ 2
Ⓓ 6

---

1. In alphabetical order, which one would be first? Fill in the circle under your answer.

Ⓐ   Ⓑ   Ⓒ   Ⓓ

---

2. In alphabetical order, which one will be last?

Ⓐ   Ⓑ   Ⓒ   Ⓓ

---

3. In alphabetical order, which one would be in the middle?

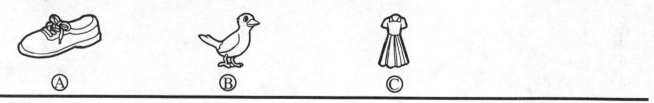

Ⓐ   Ⓑ   Ⓒ

---

4. Look at the first shape in the row. Which one of the other shapes looks like it? Fill in the circle under your answer.

Ⓐ   Ⓑ   Ⓒ   Ⓓ

---

5. If you cut on the dotted line, which one will make two triangles?

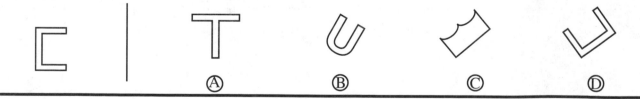

Ⓐ   Ⓑ   Ⓒ   Ⓓ

6. If you cut on the dotted line, which one will make two equal parts?

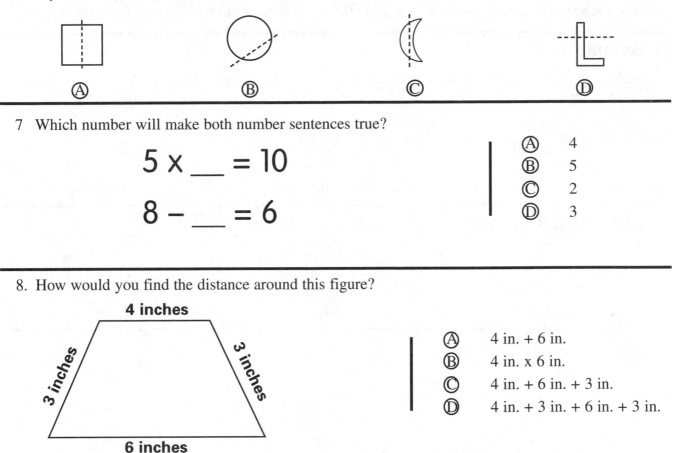

Ⓐ   Ⓑ   Ⓒ   Ⓓ

7   Which number will make both number sentences true?

$$5 \times \underline{} = 10$$

$$8 - \underline{} = 6$$

Ⓐ   4
Ⓑ   5
Ⓒ   2
Ⓓ   3

8. How would you find the distance around this figure?

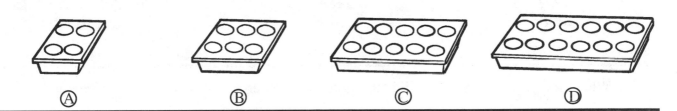

Ⓐ   4 in. + 6 in.
Ⓑ   4 in. x 6 in.
Ⓒ   4 in. + 6 in. + 3 in.
Ⓓ   4 in. + 3 in. + 6 in. + 3 in.

9. Lupe and Kelly each decorated 6 eggs. They want to display them together. Which container will hold all of their eggs? Fill in the circle next to your answer.

Ⓐ   Ⓑ   Ⓒ   Ⓓ

10. Lauren read five books. Andrew read five books. Spencer read three books. How could you show this as a number sentence?

Ⓐ   5 + 2 + 3
Ⓑ   5 x 2 + 3
Ⓒ   5 x 5 + 3
Ⓓ   5 + 1 x 3

Science: Process

Directions: This is the science part of the test. You will answer questions about temperature, size, and things you see. Read each question, and fill in the circle of your answer. Here is a sample.

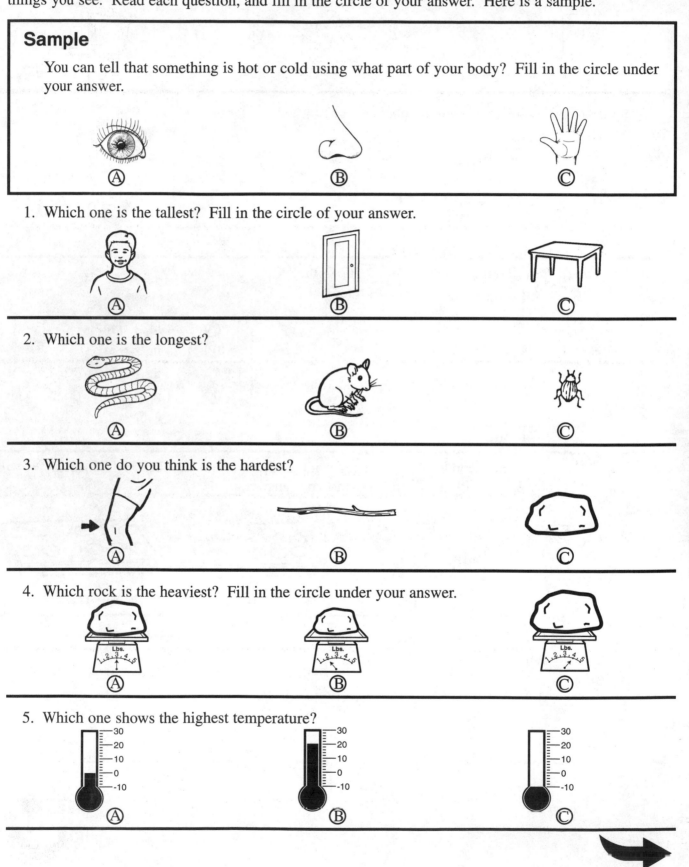

Sample

You can tell that something is hot or cold using what part of your body? Fill in the circle under your answer.

Ⓐ   Ⓑ   Ⓒ

1. Which one is the tallest? Fill in the circle of your answer.

Ⓐ   Ⓑ   Ⓒ

2. Which one is the longest?

Ⓐ   Ⓑ   Ⓒ

3. Which one do you think is the hardest?

Ⓐ   Ⓑ   Ⓒ

4. Which rock is the heaviest? Fill in the circle under your answer.

Ⓐ   Ⓑ   Ⓒ

5. Which one shows the highest temperature?

Ⓐ   Ⓑ   Ⓒ

6. Which one would have the lowest temperature?

Ⓐ   Ⓑ   Ⓒ

7. Which box would hold the most crayons?

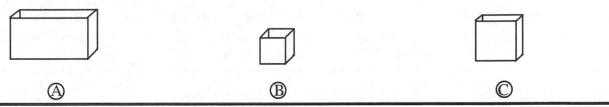

Ⓐ   Ⓑ   Ⓒ

8. Which one would hold the most water?

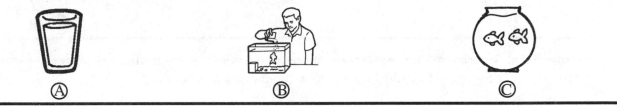

Ⓐ   Ⓑ   Ⓒ

9. Pretend you left a cold drink outside on a hot day. Later, the ice was gone. What happened?

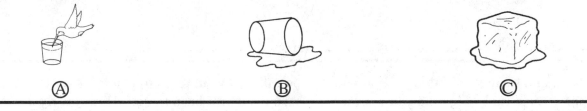

Ⓐ   Ⓑ   Ⓒ

10. Holly bought a balloon. It floated and pulled a little on its string. Then, she let the string go. What happened to the balloon? Fill in the circle under your answer.

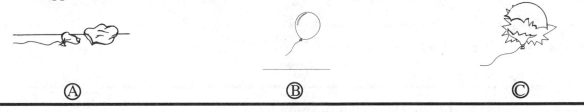

Ⓐ   Ⓑ   Ⓒ

11. Here is a fish bowl about half full of water. Someone dropped a ball in the fishbowl. What would fishbowl look like after the ball has been dropped in it?

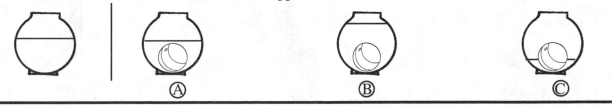

Ⓐ   Ⓑ   Ⓒ

12. Carson was making muffins. He poured them in a muffin tray. He put the tray in the oven. He forgot to turn the oven on. What will the muffins look like when he takes them out?

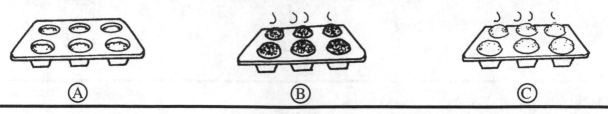

13. Andrew came running down the street. "I could tell you were baking cookies," he told his mom. "How could you tell?" said his mother. "You were so far away." How could Andrew tell his mother was baking cookies? Fill in the circle of your answer.

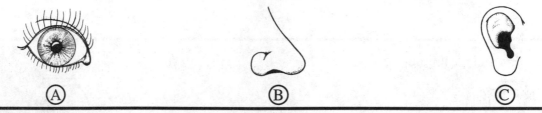

14. Lauren said to Kristen, "Let's go! The parade is starting." Kristen said, "How do you know? I can't see it coming." How did Lauren know the parade was coming?

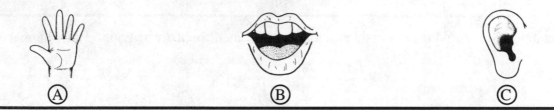

15. Kyle and Luke were hiking. Kyle said, "I don't think I want to go to that hill over there. It's too far." Luke said, "How do you know it's far? You've never been there." How did Kyle know it was far to the hill?

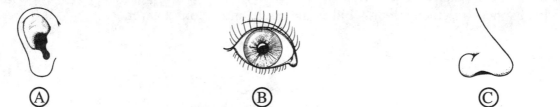

16. Which one shows the thermometer after it was in ice water?

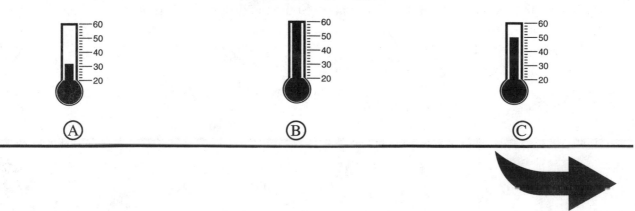

Jellybean Colors in One Pound

Color	Amount
black	10
green	16
red	30
yellow	19
white	26
orange	20

Scale: 0, 10, 20, 30

17. Mr. Anderson's class is finding out which colors of jellybeans are most often found in a one-pound bag of jellybeans. Look at the graph. Which color jellybean was found the most? Fill in the circle of your answer.

    yellow   red   white

     Ⓐ   Ⓑ   Ⓒ

18. Which color jellybean was found the least?

    black   green   red

     Ⓐ   Ⓑ   Ⓒ

Use the chart to answer questions 19 and 20.

Name	Books Read
Holly	6
Tiffany	4
Lauren	7
Kristin	3
Kyle	5
Heidi	5
Andrew	8
Dustin	2

19. Look at the chart. Who read the most books?

Ⓐ Holly
Ⓑ Lauren
Ⓒ Andrew

20. Look at the chart again. Who read the same number of books?

  Holly and Tiffany   Kyle and Heidi   Andrew and Holly

      Ⓐ   Ⓑ   Ⓒ

STOP

Science: Life, Physical, and Earth Sciences

Part I

Directions: This part of the test is about science. Read each question, and fill in the circle of your answer. Here is a sample question.

Sample

Fall, winter, summer, and spring are

Ⓐ ages.
Ⓑ seasons.
Ⓒ days.
Ⓓ temperatures.

---

1. All living things need

   Ⓐ seed.
   Ⓑ energy.
   Ⓒ soil.
   Ⓓ leaves.

2. Seeds grow in a part of a plant called a

   Ⓐ root.
   Ⓑ stem.
   Ⓒ leaf.
   Ⓓ flower.

3. You can tell a tree's age by its

   Ⓐ height.
   Ⓑ rings.
   Ⓒ bark.
   Ⓓ roots.

4. All plants and animals

   Ⓐ are straight.
   Ⓑ are green.
   Ⓒ breathe air.
   Ⓓ are useful.

5. Mold is an example of

   Ⓐ fungi.
   Ⓑ leaves.
   Ⓒ cells.
   Ⓓ dust.

6. A rose has stems and leaves. Which has scales and bones?

Ⓐ frog
Ⓑ cat
Ⓒ fish
Ⓓ human

---

7. Animals without backbones are called

Ⓐ vertebrates.
Ⓑ invertebrates.
Ⓒ environments.
Ⓓ monerans.

---

8. How does a butterfly change?

Ⓐ A moth turns into a butterfly.
Ⓑ A butterfly changes into a cocoon.
Ⓒ A caterpillar turns into a butterfly.
Ⓓ A butterfly flies south.

---

9. A human eye is most like

Ⓐ a camera.
Ⓑ a flashlight.
Ⓒ a television.
Ⓓ a mirror.

---

10. Which is a human organ?

Ⓐ skull
Ⓑ blood
Ⓒ teeth
Ⓓ heart

---

11. What pumps blood to all parts of the body?

Ⓐ heart
Ⓑ blood
Ⓒ skin
Ⓓ hair

Days from Seed to Harvest

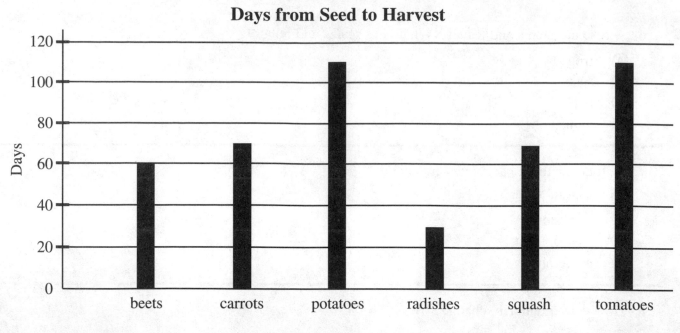

Kyle is planning a vegetable garden. He uses this bar graph to help him.

12. How long does it take carrots to grow?

   Ⓐ   60 days
   Ⓑ   70 days
   Ⓒ   65 days
   Ⓓ   61 days

13. Which vegetable will be ready the soonest?

   Ⓐ   beets
   Ⓑ   carrots and squash
   Ⓒ   radishes
   Ⓓ   potatoes and tomatoes

14. Which vegetables should Kyle plant first to make sure they have enough time to grow?

   Ⓐ   radishes
   Ⓑ   beets
   Ⓒ   carrots and squash
   Ⓓ   potatoes and tomatoes

15. Which vegetable could Kyle plant and harvest about three times before the last vegetables were ready?

   Ⓐ   radishes
   Ⓑ   beets
   Ⓒ   squash
   Ⓓ   potatoes and tomatoes

16. A fish eating a plant, and a bear eating the fish, is an example of

Ⓐ the forest.
Ⓑ calories.
Ⓒ hunting.
Ⓓ the food chain.

17. Vitamin C is mostly in fruits and vegetables. Which food would have Vitamin C?

Ⓐ a glass of chocolate milk
Ⓑ a bowl of cereal
Ⓒ a glass of orange juice
Ⓓ a dish of peanuts

18. Which is not one of the common states of matter?

Ⓐ solid.
Ⓑ liquid.
Ⓒ gas.
Ⓓ frozen.

19. Which would a magnet be attracted to?

Ⓐ salt
Ⓑ iron
Ⓒ sand
Ⓓ granite

20. Which is not a category of rock?

Ⓐ igneous
Ⓑ sedimentary
Ⓒ diamond
Ⓓ metamorphic

21. When liquid gains enough heat, it

Ⓐ melts.
Ⓑ changes to a gas.
Ⓒ freezes.
Ⓓ becomes an element.

22. Which is not a good conductor of electricity?

    Ⓐ rubber
    Ⓑ steel
    Ⓒ water
    Ⓓ copper

23. A puddle of water in the sun will

    Ⓐ dissolve.
    Ⓑ change to a solution.
    Ⓒ evaporate.
    Ⓓ spread.

24. How is dry ice used?

    Ⓐ to keep food dry
    Ⓑ to keep food warm
    Ⓒ to keep food cold
    Ⓓ to cook food

25. The center of the solar system is

    Ⓐ Earth.
    Ⓑ the sun.
    Ⓒ the Milky Way.
    Ⓓ the universe.

26. How long is a day on Earth?

    Ⓐ 12 hours
    Ⓑ 24 hours
    Ⓒ 10 hours
    Ⓓ 8 hours

27. The force that causes objects to fall and makes the ocean tides is

    Ⓐ the sun.
    Ⓑ power.
    Ⓒ gravity.
    Ⓓ motion.

28. Which is an example of a simple machine?

    Ⓐ a car
    Ⓑ a hammer
    Ⓒ a pulley
    Ⓓ a microwave

29. Magnetic force on Earth is strongest

    Ⓐ in the oceans.
    Ⓑ at the North and South poles.
    Ⓒ near volcanoes.
    Ⓓ opposite the moon.

30. The center of the Earth is called its

    Ⓐ mantle.
    Ⓑ lava.
    Ⓒ crust.
    Ⓓ core.

31. Thick layers of rotted trees and plants in tropical swamps form

    Ⓐ granite.
    Ⓑ marble.
    Ⓒ lava.
    Ⓓ coal.

32. The average weather of a region over a long period of time is

    Ⓐ cloud cover.
    Ⓑ humidity.
    Ⓒ climate.
    Ⓓ atmosphere.

Part II

Directions: Read the passage and the questions about the passage. Fill in the circle of your answer.

Fossil Clues

Scientists study the fossils in rocks. Fossils tell how old the rocks are. Fossils also give clues about what happened in the Earth's history. Fossils are mainly found in rock that was mud millions of years ago.

Most fossils are of animals with shells and tiny parts of plants and animals. Some fossils are so small scientists must look at them under a microscope. The tiny ones are the kind scientists study most.

Fossils make many people think of dinosaurs. Dinosaurs are in books, movies, and television programs. The bones and large fossils of some dinosaurs are in museums.

Dinosaurs lived on Earth for well over 100 million years. Many dinosaurs were quite small. But some weighed as much as 80 tons! Around 65 million years ago, all dinosaurs were extinct. Why they disappeared, and why they disappeared so quickly, is still not known. Maybe fossils will give us the answer.

---

33. Which is not true?

ⓐ Some fossils are of dinosaurs.
ⓑ All fossils are huge.
ⓒ Fossils give clues to the history of the Earth.
ⓓ Fossils are in rock that used to be mud.

---

34. Which is a mystery?

ⓐ why there were dinosaurs
ⓑ why so many fossils are small
ⓒ why dinosaurs disappeared
ⓓ why some animals had shells

---

35. Which is not a fact?

ⓐ Some dinosaurs weighed 80 tons.
ⓑ Dinosaurs are interesting.
ⓒ Dinosaurs lived millions of years ago.
ⓓ Dinosaurs became extinct.

Social Studies: Citizenship, Authority, and Responsibility

Directions: This is the social studies part of the test. In this part there will be questions about living in the United States. Read the question, and fill in the circle of your answer. Here is a sample.

Sample

Which is the flag of the United States of America?

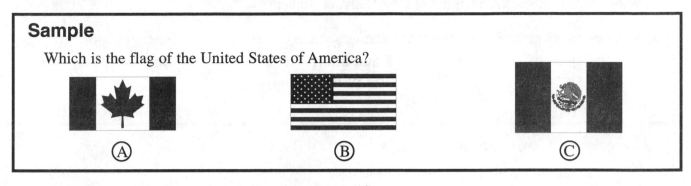

1. Which picture shows boys and girls saying the Pledge of Allegiance?

2. Which picture shows a person being a good citizen on election day?

3. Which picture shows a boy using his hat the right way when the United States flag is raised?

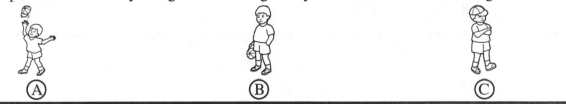

4. Which picture shows someone being a good citizen in the community?

5. Which picture shows children coming into school the right way?

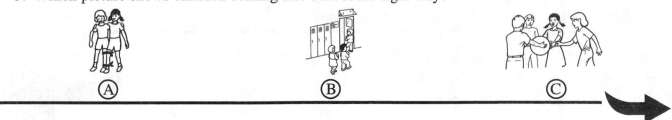

6. Which words are at the beginning of the National Anthem?

"Columbia, the gem of the ocean"	"Mine eyes have seen the glory . . ."	"O, say can you see?"
Ⓐ	Ⓑ	Ⓒ

7. Anne does not have a pencil for class. What should she do?

Ⓐ Wait until the teacher tells her to bring one.
Ⓑ Ask to borrow a pencil no one is using.
Ⓒ Bring a pencil to school.

8. CD players are not allowed at school. Kevin likes music. What should he do?

Ⓐ Keep a CD player in his backpack for private listening.
Ⓑ Leave his CD player at home.
Ⓒ Keep the CD player in his locker at all times.

9. No students are allowed to make phone calls during class. There is a substitute in Mrs. Anders room. Arthur wants to make a non-emergency call. What should he do?

Ⓐ Tell the substitute he is allowed to make calls.
Ⓑ Ask to use the bathroom and make a call instead.
Ⓒ Wait until after class to call.

10. A dog followed Bryan to school. Pets are not allowed inside. What should Bryan do?

Ⓐ Tie the dog up outside until recess.
Ⓑ Leave the dog alone.
Ⓒ Try to find the dog's home and miss school.

11. Nadine found a cigarette lighter on the sidewalk near the school. Cigarette lighters are not allowed in school. What should she do?

Ⓐ Tell an adult at school and have the adult handle it.
Ⓑ Bring it in the school and throw it away.
Ⓒ Put it in her backpack and take it home later.

12. Coach Nelson is the basketball referee. Margaret does not think Coach Nelson is being fair during the game. What should she do?

   Ⓐ Accept Coach Nelson's decisions.

   Ⓑ Ignore what he says.

   Ⓒ Refuse to play.

13. Students must remain on the playground. Stuart is playing in the outfield for baseball during recess. A ball is hit into a nearby store parking lot. What should Stuart do?

   Ⓐ Run after the ball.

   Ⓑ Tell the teacher or coach.

   Ⓒ Pretend he did not see where it went.

14. David got hit with a snowball on the playground. No snowball throwing is allowed. What should he do?

   Ⓐ Tell the teacher if it happens again.

   Ⓑ Ask who did it and threaten the person.

   Ⓒ Wait until no one is looking, and throw a snowball.

15. Marvin makes candles at home. He wants to sell them. Selling things is not allowed at school. What should he do?

   Ⓐ Sell them out of his locker only.

   Ⓑ Bring a sample candle and see if anyone wants to buy some more.

   Ⓒ Tell friends to stop by his house if they want to see or buy his candles.

16. Students must stay seated on the bus. As the bus was moving, Henry's quarter rolled to the back of the bus. What should he do?

   Ⓐ Tell the bus driver to stop the bus.

   Ⓑ Wait until the bus stops to let someone off and then quickly look for the quarter.

   Ⓒ Stay seated and tell the bus driver that he lost a quarter.

Social Studies: Religious and Cultural Traditions

Directions: This is another part of the social studies test. In this part there will be questions about traditions in the United States. Read the question, and fill in the circle of your answer. Here is a sample.

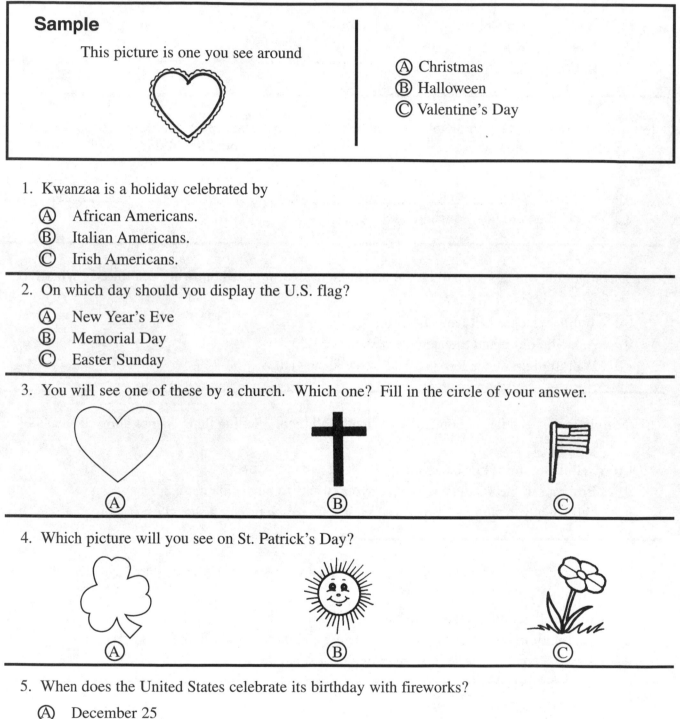

Sample

This picture is one you see around

Ⓐ Christmas
Ⓑ Halloween
Ⓒ Valentine's Day

1. Kwanzaa is a holiday celebrated by

   Ⓐ African Americans.
   Ⓑ Italian Americans.
   Ⓒ Irish Americans.

2. On which day should you display the U.S. flag?

   Ⓐ New Year's Eve
   Ⓑ Memorial Day
   Ⓒ Easter Sunday

3. You will see one of these by a church. Which one? Fill in the circle of your answer.

   Ⓐ   Ⓑ   Ⓒ

4. Which picture will you see on St. Patrick's Day?

   Ⓐ   Ⓑ   Ⓒ

5. When does the United States celebrate its birthday with fireworks?

   Ⓐ December 25
   Ⓑ January 1
   Ⓒ July 4

Social Studies: Religious and Cultural Traditions *(cont.)*

6. Which one of the pictures in this row might you see on Halloween?

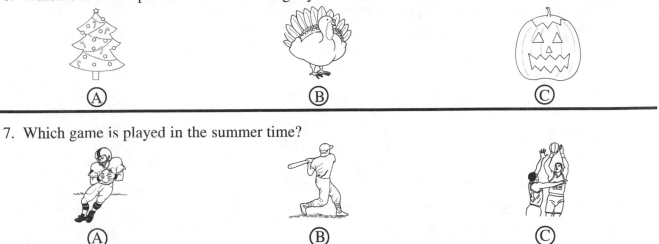

7. Which game is played in the summer time?

8. Which is the picture of the first president, George Washington?

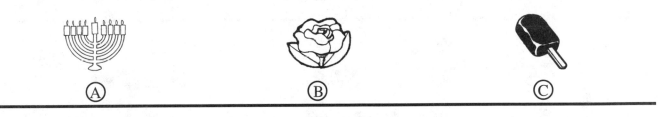

9. Which one of these is used by people who are Jewish to celebrate Hanukkah?

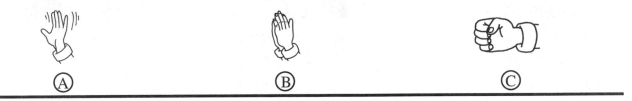

10. Which picture shows what people do with their hands when they pray?

11. Here are more pictures of hands. Which one shows a hand shake?

Social Studies: Religious and Cultural Traditions *(cont.)*

12. Which picture shows the Statue of Liberty?

Ⓐ   Ⓑ   Ⓒ

13. Which is a picture of the national bird?

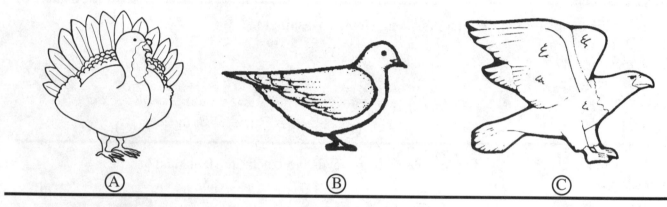

Ⓐ   Ⓑ   Ⓒ

14. Who was a leader who fought for fairness for Americans of all races?

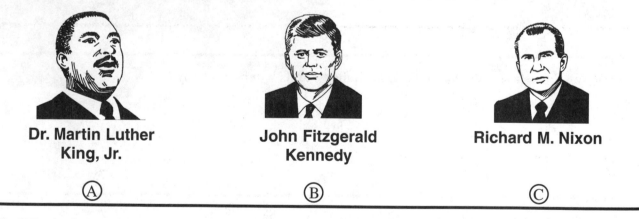

Dr. Martin Luther King, Jr.   **John Fitzgerald Kennedy**   **Richard M. Nixon**

Ⓐ   Ⓑ   Ⓒ

15. Who is the president of the United States now. Write the person's name on the line.

_____

Social Studies: Government

Directions: This part of the test is about law and government. Fill in the circle under the word that matches its definition. Here is a sample.

Sample

term

Ⓐ   Ⓑ   Ⓒ   Ⓓ

Definitions

A. throne
B. how long an elected person is in office
C. judges and courts
D. reason

---

1. **Congress**

Ⓐ   Ⓑ   Ⓒ   Ⓓ

2. **President**

Ⓐ   Ⓑ   Ⓒ   Ⓓ

Definitions

A. chief executive
B. where representatives and senators serve
C. a decision for or against
D. time of voting

3. **vote**

Ⓐ   Ⓑ   Ⓒ   Ⓓ

4. **election**

Ⓐ   Ⓑ   Ⓒ   Ⓓ

---

5. **parties**

Ⓐ   Ⓑ   Ⓒ   Ⓓ

6. **House**

Ⓐ   Ⓑ   Ⓒ   Ⓓ

Definitions

A. a run for office
B. for state representatives
C. two from each state
D. political groups like Republicans and Democrats

7. **Senator**

Ⓐ   Ⓑ   Ⓒ   Ⓓ

8. **campaign**

Ⓐ   Ⓑ   Ⓒ   Ⓓ

Matching

9. **federal**

   Ⓐ   Ⓑ   Ⓒ   Ⓓ

10. **laws**

    Ⓐ   Ⓑ   Ⓒ   Ⓓ

Definitions

A. the national government
B. rules to protect rights
C. person with the right to vote
D. money to support government services

11. **taxes**

    Ⓐ   Ⓑ   Ⓒ   Ⓓ

12. **citizen**

    Ⓐ   Ⓑ   Ⓒ   Ⓓ

Social Studies: Geography

Directions: This part of the test is about geography. Read the question, and fill in the circle of your answer. Here is a sample question.

Samples

A. Which is not a state?

- Ⓐ Wyoming
- Ⓑ Maine
- Ⓒ New Mexico
- Ⓓ Chicago

B. A major industry of the Midwest is

- Ⓐ agriculture.
- Ⓑ Illinois, Ohio, Wisconsin, Iowa, and Michigan.
- Ⓒ fishing.
- Ⓓ the Civil War.

---

1. How would you best describe a continent?

- Ⓐ mountains, valleys, and streams
- Ⓑ a globe
- Ⓒ a large land mass
- Ⓓ a point on a map

---

2. Which pair would not be helpful when reading a map?

- Ⓐ latitude and longitude
- Ⓑ equator and prime meridian
- Ⓒ degrees and days
- Ⓓ Eastern Hemisphere and Western Hemisphere

---

3. Which of the following are not landforms?

- Ⓐ mountains and valleys
- Ⓑ hills and plains
- Ⓒ boundaries and state lines
- Ⓓ islands and rivers

---

4. You could not use a map or globe for

- Ⓐ finding your location on the planet.
- Ⓑ finding out about the culture of a country.
- Ⓒ finding which continent is the smallest.
- Ⓓ finding the countries in Europe.

5. On a climate map, you would expect to see

   Ⓐ pictures of animals.

   Ⓑ temperature.

   Ⓒ favorite vacation spots.

   Ⓓ depths of water.

6. The number of people in a region is its

   Ⓐ population.

   Ⓑ census.

   Ⓒ democracy.

   Ⓓ mass.

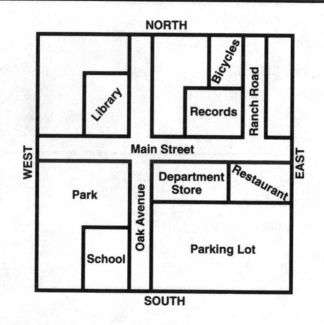

7. You are walking west on Main Street. What is on your left after you cross Oak Avenue?

   Ⓐ the library

   Ⓑ the department store

   Ⓒ the park

   Ⓓ the restaurant

8. From which street could you enter the parking lot?

   Ⓐ Oak Avenue

   Ⓑ Main Street

   Ⓒ Ranch Road

Tips for Parents: Help Your Child to Write Well

Children must be ready to learn from the first day of school. Preparing children for school is an important responsibility of parents.

Should you help your child with writing? Yes, if you want your child to do well in school, enjoy self-expression, and become more self-reliant. You know how important writing will be to your child's life. It will be important from first grade through college and throughout adulthood. After all, writing is . . .

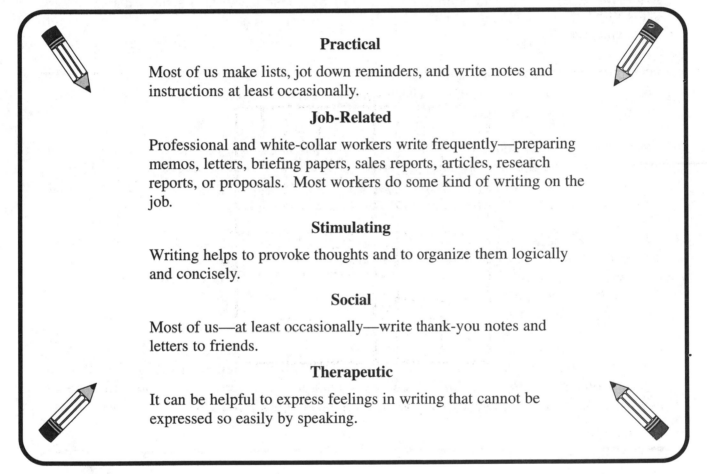

Practical

Most of us make lists, jot down reminders, and write notes and instructions at least occasionally.

Job-Related

Professional and white-collar workers write frequently—preparing memos, letters, briefing papers, sales reports, articles, research reports, or proposals. Most workers do some kind of writing on the job.

Stimulating

Writing helps to provoke thoughts and to organize them logically and concisely.

Social

Most of us—at least occasionally—write thank-you notes and letters to friends.

Therapeutic

It can be helpful to express feelings in writing that cannot be expressed so easily by speaking.

How You Can Help

1. **Encourage your child to draw and to discuss his or her drawings.** One of the first means of communication for your child is through drawing. Ask questions such as the following: *What is the boy doing? Does the house look like ours? Can you tell a story about this picture?*

2. **Show an interest in and ask questions about the things your child says, draws, and may try to write.** Most children's basic speech patterns are formed by the time they enter school. By that time, children speak clearly, recognize most letters of the alphabet, and may try to write.

3. **Make it real.** Your child also needs to do real writing. It is more important for the child to write a letter to a relative than it is to write a one-line note on a greeting card. Encourage your child to write to relatives and friends. Perhaps your child would enjoy corresponding with a pen pal.

Tips for Parents: Help Your Child to Write Well *(cont.)*

How You Can Help *(cont.)*

4. **Suggest note-taking.** Encourage your child to take notes on trips or outings and to describe what he or she saw. This could include a description of nature walks, a boat ride, a car trip, or other events that lend themselves to note-taking.

5. **Brainstorm.** Talk with your child as much as possible about his/her impressions, and encourage your child to describe people and events to you. If your child's description is especially accurate and colorful, say so.

6. **Write together.** Have your child help you with letters, even such routine ones as ordering items from an advertisement or writing to a business firm. This helps your child to see firsthand that writing is important and truly useful.

7. **Use games.** There are numerous games and puzzles that help a child to increase vocabulary and make a child more fluent in speaking and writing. Remember that building a vocabulary builds confidence. Try crossword puzzles, word games, anagrams, and cryptograms designed especially for children. Flash cards are good, too, and they are easy to make at home.

8. **Suggest making lists.** Most children like to make lists just as they like to count. Making lists is good practice and helps a child to become more organized. Boys and girls might make lists of their records, tapes, baseball cards, dolls, furniture in a room, etc. They could include items they want. It is also good practice to make lists of things to do, schoolwork, dates for tests, social events, and other reminders.

9. **Encourage copying.** If a child likes a particular song, suggest learning the words by writing them down—replaying the song on your CD player or jotting down the words whenever the song is played on a radio program. Also encourage copying favorite poems or quotations from books and plays. Overall, if you show a positive and interested attitude toward writing, your child will, too.

I liked the beach.

The sand was hot.

Tips for Parents: Help Your Child with Math

It is highly likely that when you studied math, you were expected to complete lots of problems accurately and quickly. There was only one way to arrive at your answers, and it was believed that the best way to improve math ability was to do more problems and to do them fast. Today, the focus is less on the quantity of memorized problems and more on understanding the concepts and applying thinking skills to arrive at an answer. While accuracy is always important, a wrong answer may help you and your child discover what your child may not understand. You might find some of the following thoughts helpful when thinking about wrong answers.

- **Realize problems can be solved in different ways.** While problems in math may have only one solution, there may be many ways to get the right answer. When working on math problems with your child, ask, "Could you tell me how you got that answer?" Your child's way might be different from yours. If the answer is correct and the strategy or way of solving it has worked, it is a great alternative. By encouraging children to talk about what they are thinking, we help them to become stronger mathematicians and independent thinkers.

- **Realize doing math in your head is important.** Have you ever noticed that today very few people take their pencil and paper out to solve problems in the grocery, fast food, or department store or in the office? Instead, most people estimate in their heads. Calculators and computers demand that people put in the correct information and that they know if the answers are reasonable. Usually, people look at the answer to determine if it makes sense, applying the math in their heads to the problem. This is the reason why doing math in their heads is so important to our children as they enter the 21st century.

How You Can Help

1. **Help your child do mental math with lots of small numbers in their heads until they develop quick and accurate responses.** Questions such as, "If I have 4 cups, and I need 7 cups, how many more do I need?" or "If I need 12 drinks for the class, how many packages of 3 drinks will I need to buy?"

2. **Encourage your child to estimate the answer.** When estimating, try to use numbers to make it easy to solve problems quickly in your head to determine a reasonable answer. For example, when figuring 18 plus 29, an easy way to get a "close" answer is to think about $20 + 30 = [?]$.

Tips for Parents: Help Your Child with Math *(cont.)*

How You Can Help *(cont.)*

3. **Allow your child to use strategies that make sense to him or her.** Ask often, "Is your answer reasonable? Is it reasonable that you added 17 and 35 and got 367? Why? Why not?"

4. **Ask your child to explain how the problem was solved.** The response might help you discover if your child needs help with the procedures, the number facts, or the concepts involved. Sometimes the wrong answer to a problem might be because the child thinks the problem is asking another question. For example, when children see the problem $4 + \_\_ = 9$, they often respond with an answer of 13. They think the problem is asking "What is $4 + 9$?" instead of "4 plus what missing number amount equals 9?"

   You may have learned something your child's teacher might find helpful. A short note or call will alert the teacher to possible ways of helping your child.

5. **Help your child be a risk taker.** Help him or her see the value of examining a wrong answer, and assure him or her that the right answers will come with proper understanding.

6. **Emphasize that math is enjoyable and practical.** Math is part of the everyday world. Even when you are at a fast-food restaurant, point to the prices on the menu and say, "Look! More numbers—they are everywhere!"

Above all, be patient. All children want to succeed. They do not want red marks or incorrect answers. They want to be proud and to make you and the teacher proud. So, the wrong answer tells you to look further, to ask questions, and to see what the wrong answer is saying about the child's understanding.

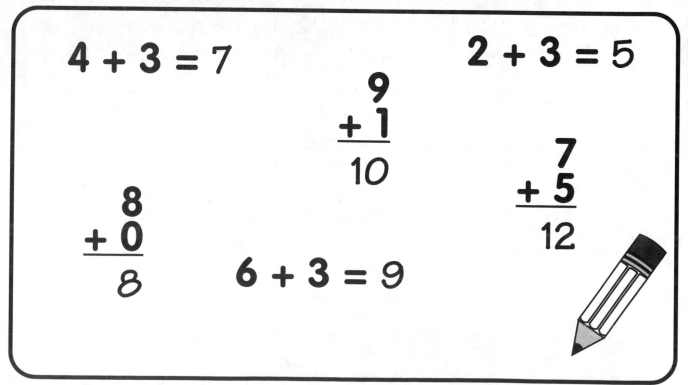

Tips for Parents: Help Your Child with Reading

You are your child's first teacher. According to the National Institute of Education, the most important thing you can do to help your child succeed in school is to read aloud to him or her. Reading to your child makes him or her feel respected and part of your world. It builds self-esteem.

Reading aloud to your child stimulates the mind, strengthens the imagination, and makes your child curious about the world. Reading aloud will help him or her to understand words, master language, and enable him or her to arrive at school feeling confident.

How You Can Help

1. **Make the reading time special.** Turn off the TV, radio, or anything that will distract from your time together. Story time can be a special part of every day—before bedtime or after a nap. Be responsive at other times, too, if your child brings a book and needs quiet time with you.

2. **Patience!** Reading to children takes time, but you will be letting them know how important they are to you. Children also love to read favorite books over and over again. Being comfortable with a book gives them confidence.

3. **Have your child choose the book you will be reading together.** Sit close together. Hold the book so your child can see it and let him or her turn the pages.

4. **Take time to look at the pictures and talk about them.** Ask your child what he or she thinks is happening or what the characters are feeling.

5. **Make the story come to life by reading with expression.** Change your voice to become different characters or to fit different situations (deep/low, quiet/soft). Ask your child to make special sounds with you—a growling animal or a howling wind.

6. **Stop at interesting points in the story and ask questions** such as "What do you think will happen next?" or "What would you do if you were there?" Help your child relate the story to his or her own experiences by asking questions like "Have you ever felt that way?" Listening to what your child has to say lets him or her know that his or her thoughts are important to you.

7. **Have fun with books and language.** Play games, sing songs, and create rhymes with your child. Read books that offer funny situations and characters so you can enjoy them and laugh together.

8. **Finally, the library can be a familiar and special place for you and your child.** Obtain a library card in your child's name. This will build self-esteem and give him or her a sense of involvement.

Test-Taking Tips

- **Read directions carefully before marking any test questions,** even though you have done that kind of test before. You may think you already know what the directions say, but don't ignore them—read them over. If you don't understand the directions, raise your hand and ask for help. Although your teacher must read the directions exactly as they are written, the teacher can make sure you understand what the directions mean.

- **Follow instructions.** Pay close attention to the sample exercises. They will help you understand what the items on the test will be like and how to mark your answer sheet properly.

- **Read the entire question and all the answer choices.** Do not stop reading when you have found a correct answer. Choices D or E may read "B and D" or "all of the above." On some tests, two answers are both correct. You need to read all the answer choices before marking your answer.

- **And remember—taking a test is not a race!** There are no prizes for finishing first. Use all of the time provided for the test. If you have time left over, check your answers.

Assessment

Assessment refers to the systematic and purposeful use of one or more of the various methods of testing student progress and achievement.

Alternative Assessment

Alternative assessment involves innovative ways of keeping track of and evaluating student work and progress. Usually contrasted with traditional, objective, standardized, norm-referenced, and paper-and-pencil testing, it includes methods such as portfolio assessment, observation of assigned tasks, and anecdotal records.

Authentic Assessment

Authentic assessment is the observation and scoring of the performance of a task in real life or, if that is impossible, in a situation that closely matches the standards and challenges of real life.

Criterion-Referenced Assessment

This kind of assessment is compared to and based upon behavioral objectives in which the learner's proficiency in an area of the curriculum is determined by his or her degree of success in completing prescribed tasks and not by comparison to the scores of other learners.

Portfolio Assessment

Portfolio assessment is a longitudinal system of assessment that occurs over a period of time and involves chronologically ordered samples of a student's work that can be compared to identify that student's progress. These samples are stored in an individual container of some kind (a portfolio).

Traditional Assessment

A traditional assessment system involves the periodic collection of data about student achievement by means of objective, standardized, norm-referenced, and paper-and-pencil tests.

Evaluation

Evaluation is the process of judging the information or results obtained from assessment for one purpose or another. (If you assess a student's ability to complete a given task in the fall and then again in the spring, you can evaluate the progress he or she has made by comparing the two assessments.)

Information Management

In an information management system, assessment information (test dates, observation checklists, portfolio materials, etc.) regarding student progress is collected, organized, and maintained.

Anecdotal Records

These used to be just lists of teacher observations stated factually and objectively without teacher interpretation or judgment. They were usually kept to document behavior problems. Anecdotal records have, however, taken on a new meaning with new forms of assessment. They have become positive narratives that document the growth and development of students. They are, at least to some extent, subjective since they contain teacher interpretation and judgment. They are often kept in student portfolios and have thus become a part of portfolio assessment

Information Management *(cont.)*

Checklists

Checklists are convenient forms in a variety of styles. They are designed (or can be designed through the use of task analysis) to help teachers record what they see during observation-based assessment.

Checkpoints

Checkpoints are important assessment points along the way between the beginning and the end of the educational process.

Exit Demonstration

Exit demonstration refers to the final culminating activity that proves that a student has mastered an area of the curriculum.

Portfolios

In addition to functioning as a type of assessment, portfolios also function as containers for collecting, organizing, and maintaining student records.

Rubrics

In connection with assessment, a rubric is a scoring guide that differentiates, on an articulated scale, among a group of student samples that respond to the same prompt.

Running Records

A running record is of student miscues (errors) made during the oral reading of a selection.

Standards

Content Standards

These are standards (frameworks; curriculum outlines) that describe the desired outcomes in various subject areas.

Curriculum Standards

The course of study in a given area; an outline of content.

National Standards

A set of standards for the whole country. Currently, a popular movement among one group of educators. Usually understood to include content standards, performance standards, and school delivery standards.

Performance Standards

Standards that define the level and quality of performance that students must exhibit to show mastery of an area of the curriculum.

School Delivery Standards

Standards that indicate whether or not a school has the resources necessary to enable students to meet the performance standards.

Tests

Tests are assessment tools constructed in such a way that achievement can be measured.

Achievement Tests

These are tests designed to assess the amount of information or degree of skill possessed by the test taker, usually objective, standardized, norm-referenced, paper-and-pencil tests.

Cognitive Tests

Cognitive tests are used to assess intellectual functioning.

Norm-Referenced Tests

These tests are based on and judged in comparison with standards determined by testing a selected pool of individuals, forming the standardized sample.

Objective Tests

Tests in which each question is stated in such a way that there is only one correct answer, true/false and multiple-choice tests are examples of objective tests.

Paper-and-Pencil Tests

We refer to tests that are designed to be read either orally by the teacher or silently by the student and answered in writing as paper-and-pencil tests.

Performance Tests

Students are asked to perform tasks while their methods and reasoning processes are observed, monitored, and recorded by means of an instrument (such as a checklist). In most cases, the students' methods and reasoning processes are considered of the same or greater value than the actual results or answers.

Proficiency Tests

Proficiency tests are written to test the objectives that are actually being taught. In order to construct a proficiency test, educators first decide on the things that they really want their students to learn (goals and objectives). Teachers then teach these things and test students to see if they have learned the material.

Psycho-Motor/Perception Tests

These tests used to measure visual-motor skills are usually standardized and norm-referenced.

Writing Sample Tests

Students are asked to demonstrate writing abilities by actually writing in response to given prompts. These writing samples are graded with the use of rubrics.

Answer Key

Language Arts: Reading
Test pages: 16–18

Test
1. Answers will vary.
2. A **B** C D
3. A **B** C D
4. A B **C** D
5. A **B** C D
6. A **B** C D
7. A B **C** D
8. A B C **D**
9. A **B** C D
10. A **B** C D
11. A B C **D**

Language Arts: Reading
Test page: 19

Sample A B **C**

Test
1. A B **C**
2. A **B** C
3. A **B** C
4. A **B** C
5. A **B** C
6. **A** B C
7. A **B** C
8. A **B** C

Language Arts: Reading
Test page: 20

Test
1. A B **C** D
2. A **B** C D
3. Answers will vary.
4. Answers will vary.
5. Answers will vary.
6. A B **C** D
7. Answers will vary.

Answer Key (cont.)

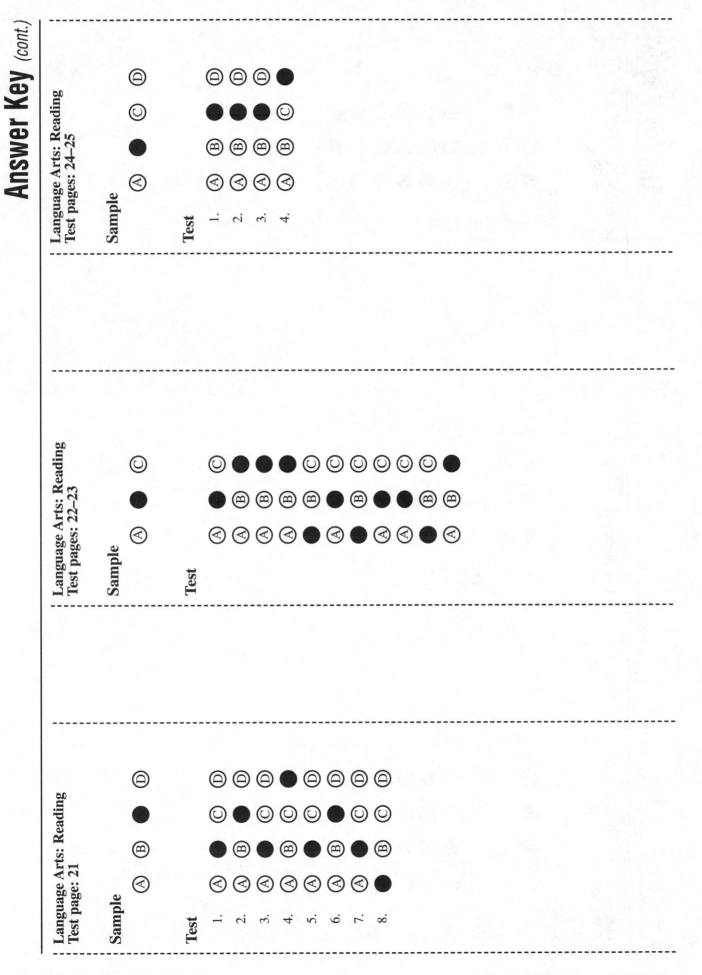

Language Arts: Reading
Test pages: 24–25

Sample: D

Test:
1. D
2. C
3. C
4. A

Language Arts: Reading
Test pages: 22–23

Sample: B

Language Arts: Reading
Test page: 21

Sample: C

Test:
1. C
2. D
3. C
4. A
5. B
6. C
7. B
8. A

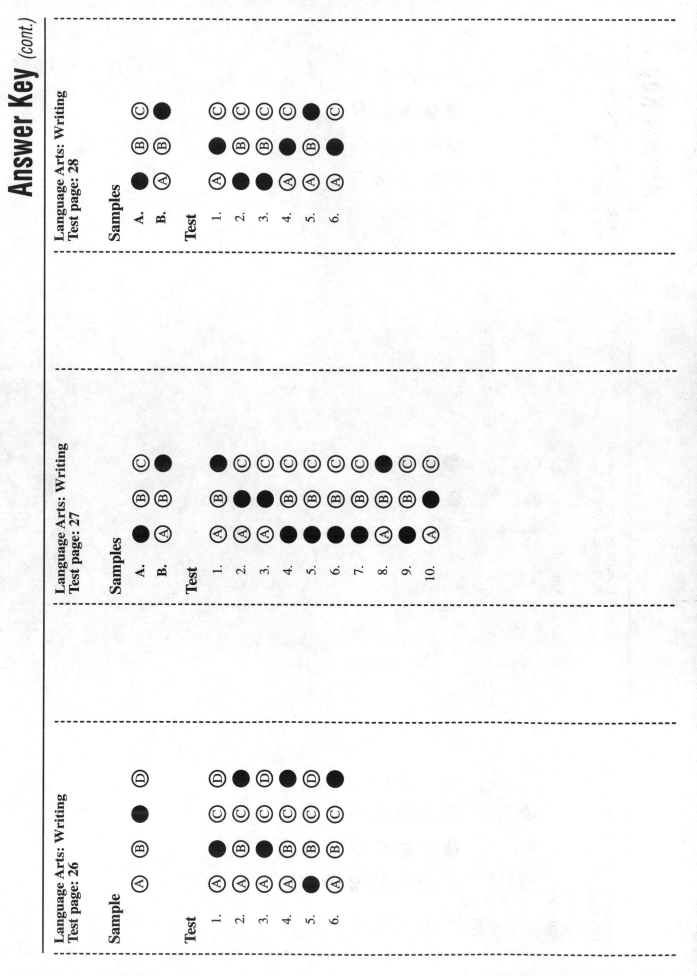

Language Arts: Writing
Test page: 28

Samples
A.
B.

Test
1.
2.
3.
4.
5.
6.

Language Arts: Writing
Test page: 27

Samples
A.
B.

Test
1.
2.
3.
4.
5.
6.
7.
8.
9.
10.

Language Arts: Writing
Test page: 26

Sample
A   B

Test
1.
2.
3.
4.
5.
6.

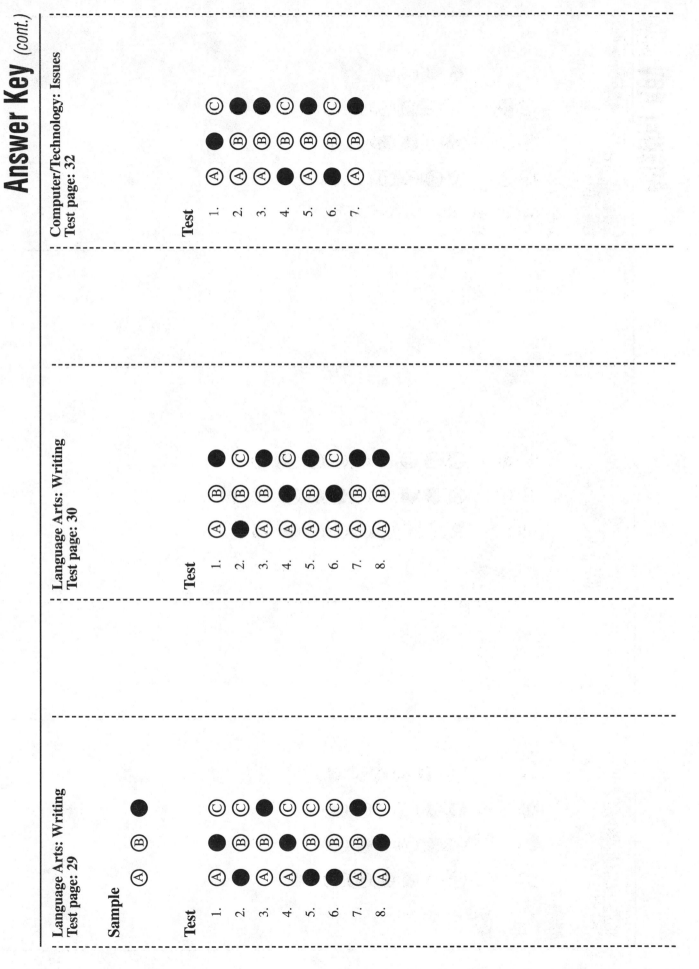

Computer/Technology: Issues
Test page: 32

Test

1. Ⓐ Ⓑ ●
2. Ⓐ Ⓑ ●
3. Ⓐ Ⓑ ●
4. ● Ⓑ Ⓒ
5. Ⓐ Ⓑ ●
6. ● Ⓑ Ⓒ
7. Ⓐ Ⓑ ●

Language Arts: Writing
Test page: 30

Test

1. Ⓐ Ⓑ ●
2. ● Ⓑ Ⓒ
3. Ⓐ Ⓑ ●
4. Ⓐ ● Ⓒ
5. Ⓐ Ⓑ ●
6. Ⓐ ● Ⓒ
7. Ⓐ Ⓑ ●
8. Ⓐ Ⓑ ●

Language Arts: Writing
Test page: 29

Sample

Ⓐ Ⓑ ●

Test

1. Ⓐ ● Ⓒ
2. ● Ⓑ Ⓒ
3. Ⓐ Ⓑ ●
4. Ⓐ ● Ⓒ
5. ● Ⓑ Ⓒ
6. ● Ⓑ Ⓒ
7. Ⓐ Ⓑ ●
8. Ⓐ ● Ⓒ

Answer Key (cont.)

Computer/Technology: Knowledge and Skills
Test page: 37

Test
1. Ⓐ Ⓑ Ⓒ ●
2. Ⓐ Ⓑ Ⓒ ●
3. Ⓐ ● Ⓒ Ⓓ
4. Ⓐ ● Ⓒ Ⓓ

Computer/Technology: Knowledge and Skills
Test pages: 35–36

Test
1. ● Ⓑ Ⓒ
2. Ⓐ ● Ⓒ
3. Ⓐ ● Ⓒ
4. Ⓐ Ⓑ ●
5. Ⓐ Ⓑ ●
6. Ⓐ ● Ⓒ
7. Ⓐ ● Ⓒ
8. ● Ⓑ Ⓒ

Computer/Technology: Issues
Test pages: 33–34

Sample
Ⓐ ● Ⓒ

Test
1. Ⓐ Ⓑ ●
2. ● or ● Ⓒ
3. ● Ⓑ Ⓒ
4. ● or ● Ⓒ
5. Ⓐ ● Ⓒ
6. Ⓐ Ⓑ ●

**Mathematics: Geometric Ideas
Test pages: 45–47**

**Mathematics: Whole Numbers
Test pages: 41–44**

**Mathematics: Whole Numbers
Test pages: 38–40**

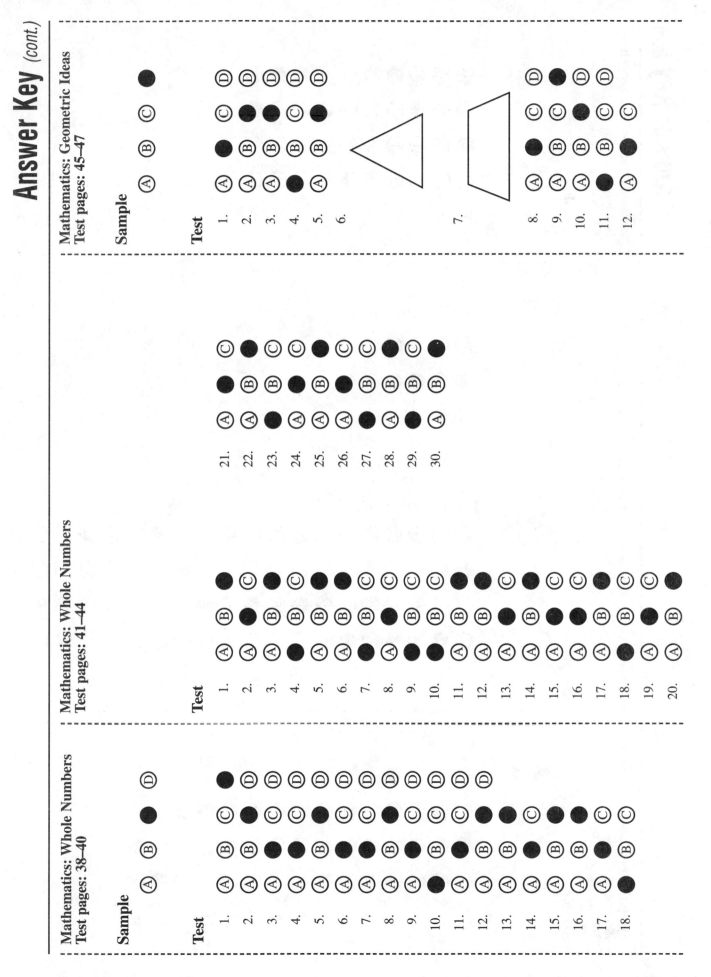

Mathematics: Classification and Pattern
Test pages: 48–50

Mathematics: Metric and Customary Measurement
Test pages: 51–55

Mathematics: Problem Solving
Test pages: 56–57

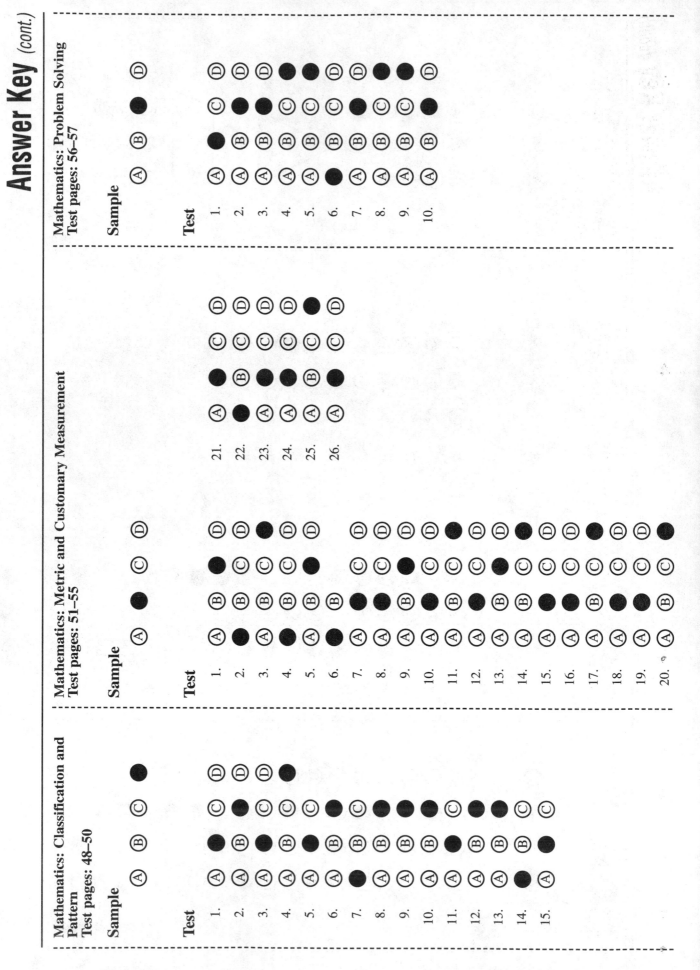

Answer Key *(cont.)*

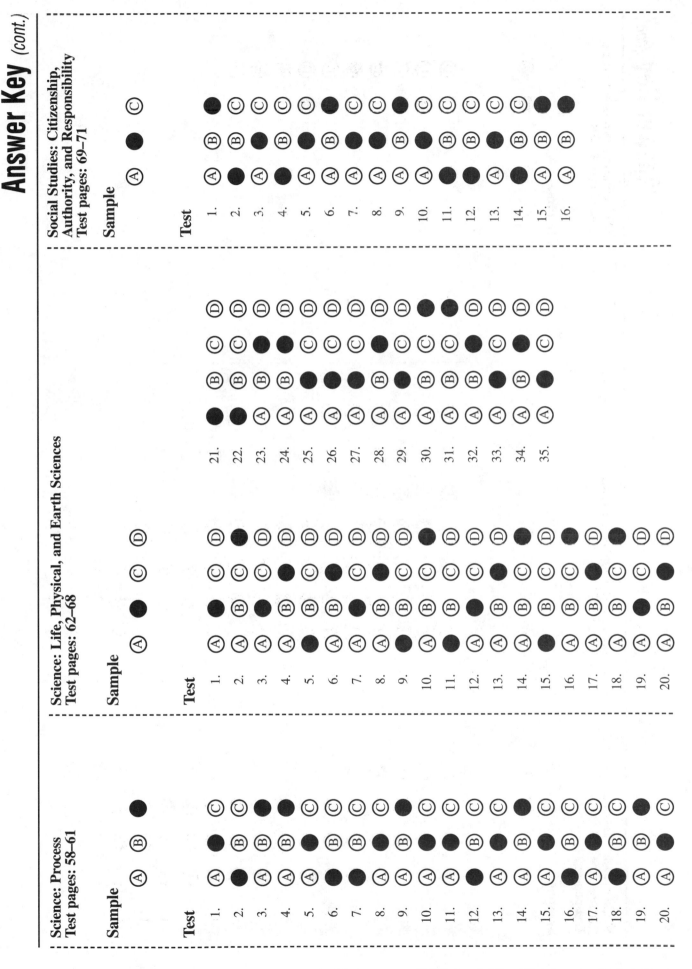

Social Studies: Citizenship, Authority, and Responsibility
Test pages: 69–71

Science: Life, Physical, and Earth Sciences
Test pages: 62–68

Science: Process
Test pages: 58–61

Social Studies: Geography
Test pages: 77–78

Samples

A.
B.

Test

1.
2.
3.
4.
5.
6.
7.
8.

Social Studies: Government
Test pages: 75–76

Sample

Test

1.
2.
3.
4.
5.
6.
7.
8.
9.
10.
11.
12.

Social Studies: Religious and
Cultural Traditions
Test pages: 72–74

Sample

Test

1.
2.
3.
4.
5.
6.
7.
8.
9.
10.
11.
12.
13.
14.
15. Name of current president.

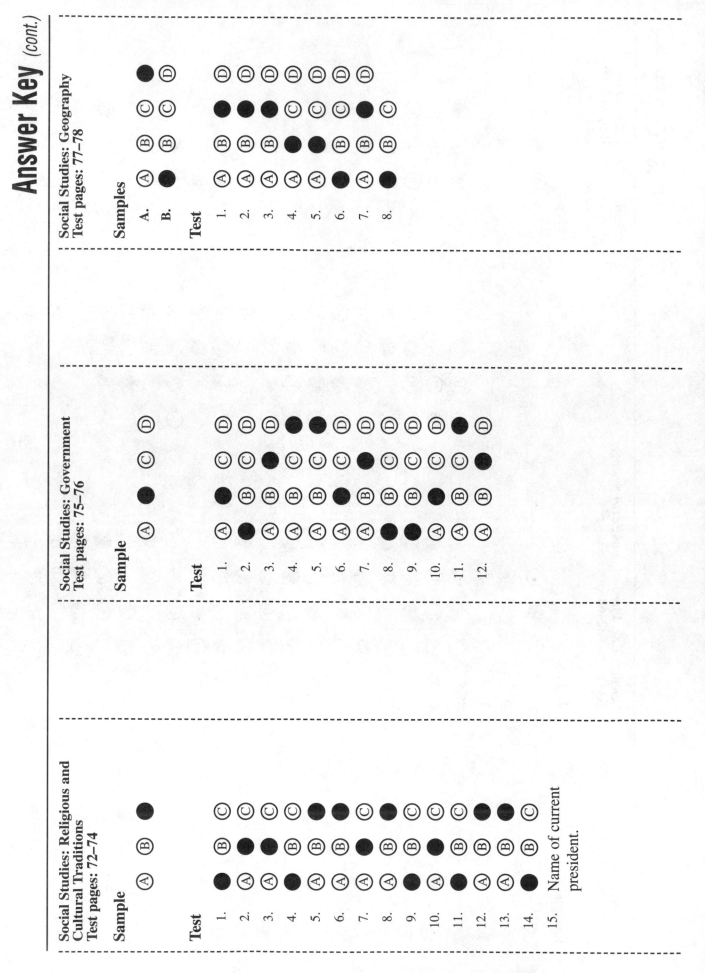